A GENERALIZED THEORY OF INTERNATIONAL TRADE

A Generalized Theory
of International Trade

H. PETER GRAY

 HOLMES & MEIER PUBLISHERS
New York

First published in the United States of America 1976 by
Holmes & Meier Publishers, Inc.
101 Fifth Avenue
New York, New York 10003

© H. Peter Gray 1976

HF 1007
G674

Library of Congress Cataloging in Publication Data

Gray, H. Peter.
    A generalized theory of international trade.

    Bibliography:
    Includes index.
    1. Commerce. 2. Commercial policy. I. Title.
HF1007.G674   1976   382.1   76-5819
ISBN 0-8419-0271-2

PRINTED IN GREAT BRITAIN

TO MY MENTORS

Contents

Preface

In many ways this book is a companion to *An Aggregate Theory of International Payments Adjustment*. Its purpose is to bring greater realism to the micro-part of international economics — the part that deals with international resource allocation. Like its companion, this book has the avowed intent of incorporating direct investment and multi-national enterprise into a body of theory that allows for it only, as it were, as an afterthought or addendum. The book also attempts to shift the emphasis of the body of theory away from elegance or potential for elegance and toward pragmatic relevance. Inevitably, this kind of theoretical construct creates more empty boxes than it fills. The theory presented here is essentially synthetic in that much of it derives from the work of other economists. Like *An Aggregate Theory*, this attempts to supplant the received doctrine by extending and broadening the orthodox into an analytic framework that will provide a better basis for diagnosis of real-world policy alternatives. Finally, it has the same obstacle to acceptance: acceptance will require international economists to tear down some of the human capital so arduously acquired.

I have already mentioned the importance of the work of others in the ideas generated here. It is for this reason that I have dedicated the book to my mentors. Most of these are mentioned in footnotes in the text and are familiar names. One person who is not mentioned was the man who first aroused my fascination with international economic analysis. If, on reading this book, Philip W. Bell is led to feel that he played an important role in creating a heretic, I hope he will at least approve the intent. In the course of the development of these ideas I benefited from comments on all or part of the manuscript from many people: Richard E. Caves, Jean M. Gray, Robert G. Hawkins, Marjorie W. Munson, H. Bart Myers, Dewey Seeto, R. M. Stearns and J. W. Wheeler. I am indebted to them but they are not responsible for the final text. My thanks are also due to the editors of *Weltwirtschaftliches Archiv* and

Economia Internazionale respectively for permission to reproduce 'Two-way International Trade in Manufactures: A
Theoretical Underpinning' (1973), pp. 19–39, and 'A Tripartite Model of International Trade' (1974), pp. 260–79. I
would also like to acknowledge the support of the Rutgers
University Research Council.

The ideas contained in these pages have had a long gestation
period. The idea of non-competitive goods first impressed its
importance upon my thinking in 1964. It was not fully
formulated until the autumn of 1968 when the first draft of the
tripartite model (Chapter 4) was written in an attempt to make
analytic sense out of international trade in tourism — a topic
which stoutly resisted being analyzed within the orthodox
framework. Since then the ideas have matured and benefited
from discussion with my students. The appendix on environmental protection owes much to many conversations with
Sharon Bernstein Megdal. Once again Mrs Doris K. Cunningham
and Mrs Gerri Dructor were invaluable in the production of the
manuscript.

H. Peter Gray

Belle Mead, New Jersey

Part One
Derivation

1 The Purpose of the Study and the Analytic Constraints

The task of economic theory is not 'to hold, as 'twere, the mirror up to nature'. The world around us is too complex and too subject to minor aberrations for a true reproduction to have analytic value. Factors such as impulse buying, transitory interruptions in supply, shortlived imperfections in markets can, together with the general overlay of stochastic disturbances and dynamic forces, complicate the analysis without offering compensating insights. Rather, the purpose of a body of economic theory is to identify the main interdependencies of the system and to isolate those interdependencies in such a way that the crucial relationships and their causal links stand out in sharp focus. The emphasis on the main causal relationships makes possible an analysis of the effect of a specified disturbance upon the working of the economic system.

There is a finite amount of complexity that can be handled at a single time by any organism, be that organism computer and econometric model or human brain and mathematical or literary model. The greater the degree of simplification of an analysis, the more readily can the effects of a disturbance on the major variables be traced out. But, the greater simplicity permits nothing to be deduced about the effects of the disturbance upon the excluded variables and, in this way, prohibits any examination of the feedback of such effects upon the included variables. The more inclusive a theory – the further down the scale of importance are the relationships that are included – the more specialized must that theory be. The need for specialization follows from the fact that to make a theory more inclusive on a general or non-specialized basis would require that every ramification of the theory be developed to the same degree of inclusiveness. Specialization notwithstanding, the more inclusive the theoretical base the greater is the inherent complexity of the analysis and, the greater the complexity, the less likely exact solutions are to be attainable or clear cause-and-effect relationships to be identifiable.[1] It is possible for a theory to become so mired down in a sea of minutiae that the analysis is worthless.

However, if complexity presents difficulty, so too does simplification. Clearly, any simplification of the real world courts the dangers of eliminating from the analytic tool-kit an element that is important to the problem at hand. The reliance of neoclassical theory upon the automatic tendency toward full employment as a reason for a lack of concern with the problems of unemployment or adjustment is an obvious case in point. For this reason, the simplifying assumptions of any body of theory must always be explicitly spelled out and an investigator must never fail positively to consider the relevance of his theoretical framework based on those assumptions for his immediate task or problem. No single theoretical model can be suitable for all conceivable analyses of such a complex phenomenon as the real world. Such a model would defy comprehension by a single organism and would frustrate the goal of theoretical analysis.

Given that both simple and complex models have their disadvantages, there exists the very real and pertinent question as to what constitutes the most appropriate degree of complexity or simplification for an analytic endeavour. Such a decision must take into account the purpose of the analysis. But to be able to consider objectively this problem of the appropriate degree of complexity, the analyst must have some concept of the way in which complexity or simplicity is achieved in economic analysis. Economic analysis addresses itself to two main questions: the level of resource utilization and the efficiency of resource utilization. The problem of simplification and of the appropriate trade-off can be considered first in terms of the macro-question of the level of resources utilization.

A theory (a model or an analytic frame of reference) consists

---

[1] Compare Richard E. Caves' statement: 'Because of the ponderous results of attacking so many variables with the more elaborate and exact of present-day theoretical tools, the following exposition runs in purely literary form' in 'Vent for Surplus Models of Trade and Growth', in R. E. Baldwin *et al.*, *Trade, Growth and the Balance of Payments* (Chicago: Rand McNally, 1965) p. 97.

of a network of interrelationships among sectors together with a set of specifications of the causal links within that network. A theory may be used for exposition, as a basis for further deduction, for hypothesis generation and associated empirical experimentation and for policy recommendations. A macroeconomic system can be defined as consisting of several main areas that are interdependent. Each of these main areas or sectors possesses its own internal interrelationships or second-generation subsectors, third-generation subsectors and so on. The distinction between a main area and a subsector is that a subsector's degree of interdependence with its fellow subsectors exceeds by a substantial margin the interdependence which it enjoys with other main sectors; this is achieved primarily on a collective basis through its own main sector.[2]

For example, the simplest Keynesian model comprises two main sectors (the private and government sectors) and two second-generation subsectors of the private sector (consumption and investment). In a world with an unemployment rate of 25 per cent and a liquidity trap, this degree of complexity could be considered sufficient. To clutter up the model with sterile variables would tend merely to reduce the starkness of the relationship between the level of government expenditures and the level of resource utilization. The standard Keynesian model deals with less drastic conditions and is complicated by the introduction of the monetary sector (main) and by the inclusion of second-generation subsectors in government (transfers, taxes and goods-and services expenditures) and by third-generation subsectors of the private sector (the subdivisions of investment and consumption).

The introduction of the structure of the monetary sector in the form of the second-generation subsectors of the commercial banking system and capital and money market institutions complicates the analysis. A change in the private sector will affect the structure of financial institutions primarily through the system of financial markets (the main sector). Individual

[2] The distinction is based, then, upon the degree of interdependence. Any entity that has a closer interdependence with a similar entity than with a distinctly different sector is a subsector. Equally, any entity that has a smaller interdependence with a distinctly different sector than does a combination of itself and other sectors is a subsector. For a mathematical treatment of interdependencies, see Richard N. Cooper, *The Economics of Interdependence* (New York: McGraw-Hill, or the Council on Foreign Relations, 1968) Ch. 5.

institutions are affected only at one remove. Changes in the structure — from a change in governmental regulations governing commercial banks, for example — will affect the way in which the monetary sector combines with other main sectors. There may be some direct interdependence among second or third-generation subsectors belonging to different main sectors but these linkages are less important than the linkages that exist among the main sectors themselves.

A second means of distinguishing between a main sector and a subsector relates to policy goals. A main sector has a goal set for it that is designed to allow the sector to make a maximum contribution to the achievement of the national economic goals of efficiency, growth, employment, price stability and income distribution. Subsectors do not have goals outlined for them in terms of their effect upon national goals; rather their goals are outlined in terms of the goal of the main sector.

The degree of complexity of a theory can be described in terms of the number of main and subsectors included in the analysis. Thus, the inclusion of a sector or subsector is very likely to involve little more than the elimination of a simplifying assumption — though not all assumptions have the same 'coefficient of simplification'. The trade-off between simplicity and complexity for macro-models is easily seen. The less inclusive the theory, the easier it is to grasp the mechanism and the more starkly do the causalities stand out. The inclusion of third-generation subsectors of various kinds will complicate the analysis but may add little light to the solution provided and may even obscure it. The more simplified the theory, the greater the danger that it will inadvertently omit some interrelationship that is vital to the purpose of the analysis. The key to inclusion or omission is clearly the quantitative importance of the relationship. Macro-economic forecasts in the United States may well have been able in the 'fifties to exclude the balance on goods and services because of its insignificance relative to the gross national product and because of its stability. However, once the current account began to fluctuate widely, its inclusion was necessary.

The second type of economic analysis is concerned with allocative efficiency. Theories portray interrelationships and causal links within a particular sector or industry or within an economy as a whole. The criteria by which the trade-off between simplicity and complexity is resolved in this type of analysis resemble their macro-economic equivalents closely. But in this type of analysis, the problem of the tradeoff is itself complicated by its duality. The theorist must decide to what degree the sector can be treated in isolation and the inter-dependencies with other (main) sectors ignored. The theorist must also decide upon the appropriate degree of complexity for the analysis of the sector in isolation. The analysis of the sector in isolation can be defined as the 'core' theory of a field. For any given level of complexity of analysis of the core theory, the greater the interdependence with other main sectors, the greater is the complexity of the total analysis. A core theory is made more complex by the disaggregation process. Such a dis-aggregation process will involve an increase in the number of species of goods included in the model as well as by an increase in the number and kinds of inputs. Complexity is enhanced if institutional detail is included and if imperfect competition is introduced. The fewer the simplifying assumptions, the less likely are exact solutions to be attained or clear cause-and-effect relationships to be identifiable.

The distinction that the preceding paragraphs have attempted to draw has recently been expressed both succinctly and lucidly:

> ... it is basically the Ricardian method of analysis that Keynes has revived. The most typical indication of this is to be found in the directness with which Keynes proceeds to state his assumptions. Like Ricardo, he is always looking for fundamentals. He singles out for consideration the variables he believes to be the most important. All the others giving rise to unimportant complications — though, as he says, are always 'kept at the back of his head' for the necessary qualifications — are, for immediate purposes, frozen out by simple assumptions.[3]

This book is concerned with the degree of complexity appropriate for the core theory of international trade. The ap-propriate degree of complexity is not subject to precise definition and each economist can, therefore, enjoy some leeway in his approach. However, the contention here is that

---

[3] L. L. Pasinetti, *Growth and Income Distribution, Essays in Economic Theory* (London: Cambridge University Press, 1974) pp. 43–4.

the received body of international trade theory is far too
simplified to serve usefully as a basis for pragmatic analysis.[4] In
its place, the book offers a more complex theory which will
serve more reliably as a basis for decisions about international
trade (and payments) policies and for analyses of real-world
problems. The more complex theory to be offered here has
been described as 'generalized'. In this context and in terms of
the preceding paragraphs, the term 'generalized' means that the
number of subsectors explicitly included in (or the number of
simplifying assumptions discarded from) the generalized theory
will be greater than the number included in (discarded from)
the so-called orthodox theory. The new theory has, therefore,
broader applicability and generality. However, it is worth
pointing out that the generalized theory is derivative rather than
original in any fundamental sense. The generalized theory will
represent the international sector (main) in macro-economic
analyses in the same way as the orthodox theory. In that
capacity, or as a core theory for international economics, it is
concerned with the problems of economic efficiency and
income distribution. The generalized theory will also have
greater applicability to the intersectoral macro-model concerned
with employment levels in that it will be capable of discarding
the assumption of balanced trade so crucial to its orthodox
counterpart.

An adequate theory of international trade should portray the
interrelationships that govern the division of production among
nations, the gain from trade, and the effect of trade upon the
domestic economies. It should also explain the variation in the
prices of commodities that occurs in different nations before
and after trade. Such a theory must be a mutual interdependence
price theory. This assertion agrees with Bertil Ohlin's contention about what he calls the *basic* model of international trade
and what is referred to here as the core theory of the field.[5]

[4] It is worth noting that, of all the main sectors, international economics is that
sector that requires the clearest statement of national economic policy. This derives
in part from the interdependence of international economic and political variables
and in part from the fact that international economic policy involves dealing with
sovereign, independent trading partners – see my *An Aggregate Theory of International Payments Adjustment* (London: Macmillan, 1974) p. 23–5.

[5] Bertil Ohlin, *Interregional and International Trade* (revised ed.), (Cambridge,
Mass.: Harvard University Press, 1966), Appendix II, 'Reflections on Contemporary
International Trade Theories' – hereafter referred to as 'Reflections' – pp. 306–7.

It is clear, then, that the philosophy underlying the generalized model is that theory is not an end in itself and can be useful only as a means to an end. Undeniably, some of the more elaborate and elegant exercises in the theory of international trade are so rarified that it would be difficult to justify their existence other than as the seeking of analytic elegance for its own sake.[6] The generalized theory will be less well suited to elegant manipulation and, while it may represent a step backward in time, it represents a step forward in methodology — as it were away from Jones and Kemp and toward Viner.[7]

There is no unanimity among international trade theorists as to what constitutes the received core theory. There is a rivalry between the factor—proportions theory and the classical theory. It is not a gross oversimplification of the state of the arts to say that the factor—proportions approach is beloved by the pure theorists but that the weight of the empirical evidence supports the classical explanation of international trade structure.[8] Until this fundamental discord has been reconciled, international trade theory is in an ambivalent position and the concept of a reigning theory is subject to some doubt. Equally, this ambivalence itself means that international trade theory is subject to challenge. The failure of *both* strands of the theory to provide any rationale for or explanation of the worldwide spread of multinational enterprise is clear evidence of their indadequacy for analysis of real-world problems.[9] Neither theory allows for international trade to take place in intermediate goods and in factor inputs and each is overburdened with the consequences of the timelessness that characterizes its solution. Of these, the implications of multinational enterprises,

[6] In this context but in monetary rather than international economics, the following sentence is extremely apt: 'He produces a catalogue which might offer less dangerous guidance to the administrator, because of making less ambitious claims, than algebraic models offering delusive exactness and resting on a mass of small print, or no print at all.' G. L. S. Shackle, review of: Paul Davidson, *Money and the Real World*, (London: Macmillan, 1972), *Economic Journal* 83, (June 1973), p. 533.

[7] Bertil Ohlin makes the same point in 'Reflections', footnote[11], p. 310 and in 'The Business Cost Account Approach to International Trade Theory,' *Swedish Journal of Economics*, (February 1970), pp. 12—13.

[8] See Richard E. Caves' summary of the relative strengths of the two theories in *Trade and Economic Structure*, (Cambridge: Harvard University Press, 1960), ch. 10 and particularly p. 282.

[9] J. H. Dunning, 'The Determinants of International Production', *Oxford Economic Papers*, (November 1973), pp. 289—336.

at least, are sufficiently important to warrant inclusion in the core theory.

To propose a new theory usually requires that the old one be dis-established. The intent of this book is to generalize the orthodox theory rather than to denigrate it. In fact, the orthodox theory – in either its factor–proportions or its classical version – is quite adequate to the task of putting the case for free trade in an equilibrium world devoid of multi-national corporations. Quite recently Willett has argued that orthodox international trade theory is still relevant in the modern world.[10] This argument was, in fact, less a defence of trade theory than a defence of a policy conclusion that derives from both strands of the traditional theory – that the limitations imposed by the assumptions do not invalidate the policy conclusion that free exchange of goods is a wise basis for international economic policy. With the possible exception of international mobility of factors of production, the weaknesses cited were not those that dominate the thinking of people concerned with the make-up of the core theory. Willett considered the possibility that money costs of goods did not reflect relative social costs, that disequilibrium rates of exchange prevailed, that neo-mercantilist policies were followed at home and abroad, and that the international mobility of capital and technology were strong enough to refute the conclusions that derive from a theory based exclusively on the exchange of goods.

The format of this book is to derive the theory in the next five chapters and to devote the remaining six chapters to applications of the theory for certain important areas in international economics. Chapter 2 is devoted to a critique of the existing theory and, in the process, identifies a model that can be taken as representative of the most narrow version of the orthodox core theory. The chapter also evaluates the main criticisms in terms of the desirability of including the facet discussed in or excluding it from the core theory being proposed. As indicated, the core theory cannot be uniquely defined in terms of the trade-off between generality and manageability. Chapter 3 introduces the concepts that are

[10] Thomas D. Willett, 'International Trade Theory is Still Relevant', Banca Nazionale del Lavoro *Quarterly Review*, (September 1971) pp. 276–92.

fundamental to the generalized theory, and that both amend the orthodox model and reconcile the two strands of orthodoxy. Chapter 4 presents the core theory in literary form and, for expository purposes, derives a minimal formal equilibrium model, which involves the use of five factors of production and five commodities. The formal model is then used to show that some of the inevitable consequences of the orthodox model no longer need apply. Chapter 5 develops the generalized theory as it applies to small adjustments; here the distinction is between general and industry-specific disturbances and between autonomous and derived disturbances. Chapter 6 develops and extends the theory by releasing some of the basic assumptions laid down in chapter 4. Transportation costs and imperfect product markets are considered. But the elimination of the assumption of balanced trade in goods and services is, together with the consideration of the effects of capital flows and unilateral transfers, a more substantial development of the generalized theory.

The application of the generalized theory allows broader insights into such phenomena as colonialism, multi-national enterprise, commercial policy and two-way trade than the orthodox theory can provide.

2 The Shortcomings of the Orthodox Theory

The classical theory of international trade postulates different production functions for identical goods in different countries and attributes comparative advantage to these differences. Its premises were under attack before the factor—proportions theory was revealed in its full maturity in 1933. Both Graham and Williams made major critiques but neither succeeded in dethroning the reigning concepts.[1] Ohlin's expansion of Heckscher's seminal paper presented a viable alternative to the classical model.[2] Since its appearance, the factor—proportions model has held centre stage despite the clear superiority of the classical model as a basis for empirical work. There have, however, been many critiques of the factor—proportions theory and these critiques have been appearing with increasing frequency. The critiques derive, in part, from the empirical shortcomings of the theory, in part from the clear lack of relevance of the theory to some major post-World War Two phenomena and, in part, from the vulnerability of some of its premises.[3] Not the least important target for criticism has been the increasingly elegant formulations of the factor—proportions theory. These formulations have progressively removed the central core of international trade theory away from Heckscher's concepts and the literary version of Ohlin's model and toward the more restrictive Casselian version.[4] The extreme

---

[1] See Frank D. Graham, 'The Theory of International Values Re-examined' and John H. Williams, 'The Theory of International Trade Reconsidered', in H. S. Ellis and L. A. Metzler (eds.), *Readings in the Theory of International Trade* (Philadelphia: Blakiston, 1950), respectively pp. 301—30 and 253—71.

[2] Bertil Ohlin, *Interregional and International Trade* (Cambridge, Mass.: Harvard University Press, 1933) and Eli Heckscher, 'The Effect of Foreign Trade on the Distribution of Income' in *Readings in the Theory of International Trade*, pp. 272—300. For an account of the dependence of Ohlin's treatise on Heckscher, see Caves, *Trade and Economic Structure*, pp. 24—30.

[3] The most comprehensive of these critiques is that of Ohlin himself: 'Reflections'.

[4] See Caves, *Trade and Economic Structure*, p. 27.

form of the factor—proportions theory can be said to be represented by Bhagwati's analysis of the two-country, two-factor, multi-commodity case in which strong factor—intensity ranking is assumed to hold and in which factor—price equalization has already been achieved.[5] Bhagwati describes the case when factor—price equalization is realized, as 'not unimportant'.[6] Given the restrictiveness of these two assumptions, the charge of excessive artificiality is quite natural. The conditions necessary for factor—price equalization are:[7]

1. Two countries are involved.
2. Two commodities are both produced and traded.
3. Both factors of production are used in both goods, and production functions are homogeneous in the first degree and hence subject to Euler's theorem.
4. The law of diminishing marginal productivity holds.
5. The production functions differ in factor intensity, that is, at a given factor—price ratio the two goods use the two factors in different proportions.
6. The production function for a given good is the same in either country; land and labour inputs are qualitatively identical.
7. There is perfect competition and no international factor mobility, and tariffs and transport costs are assumed absent.
8. In equilibrium, demand and cost conditions are such that no commodity ceases to be produced in either country.
9. Factor quantities remain constant; this is not explicitly listed by Samuelson, and indeed the proof does not depend upon it, but references to box diagrams in both the 1948 and 1949 articles strongly imply it.

The strong factor—intensity assumption is attributable to Samuelson and assumes that the ranking of goods by factor-

---

[5] Jagdish N. Bhagwati, 'The Heckscher—Ohlin Theorem in the Multi-commodity Case,' *Journal of Political Economy* 80 (September/October 1972), pp. 1052—55. It is worth noting that in his summary of the factor—proportions theory G. C. Hufbauer cites as the four central assumptions the very assumptions that make the theory stillborn: factor immobility; strong factor—intensity ranking; identical technology (production functions); and constant returns to scale. See *Synthetic Materials and the Theory of International Trade*, pp. 15—16.

[6] Bhagwati, *op. cit.*, p. 1052.

[7] The list is taken from Caves, *Trade and Economic Structure*, p. 77.

intensity is independent of the set of factor prices common to both goods.[8]

SHORTCOMINGS OF THE FACTOR-PROPORTIONS THEORY

Using the extreme version of the factor—proportions theory as a reference point, the shortcomings of the theory can be listed and can be considered sequentially. It has already been noted that the classical model has provided a more reliable base for empirical work. In this sense it is, potentially, an alternative reference point. The classical theory, creating production functions out of thin air as it does, fails to explain the causes of international trade sufficiently and fails, too, to allow for the effects of international trade on the internal workings of the economies to be derived within its frame of reference. However, in so far as it constitutes an alternative core theory based largely on differing production conditions in the two countries, the classical theory can also be seen as a criticism of the factor—proportions theory. It will be treated here in this manner. The shortcomings are listed in, approximately, increasing order of importance and tractability.

1. Intranational locational factors and impediments to the free movement of factors within a nation are assumed not to affect a nation's trading stance.
2. The international immobility of factors and fixed (or defined) factors supplies assumptions.
3. The full employment assumption that is inevitably a part of a timeless general equilibrium solution.
4. The failure to consider imperfect competition in factor and product markets.
5. The influence of taxes and social legislation upon relative factor prices and the cost of goods.
6. International transportation costs are excluded.
7. The failure to use money costs and prices.
8. Reliance on linear, homogeneous production functions excludes any consideration of scale economies.
9. Emphasis on finished goods precludes consideration of

---

[8] See R. W. Jones, 'Factor Proportions and the Heckscher—Ohlin Theorem,' *The Review of Economic Studies* 24 (1956), pp. 2 and 3. The realism of this assumption decreases as the number of factors increases.

trade in intermediate goods, technology and, hence, a *raison d'etre* for multinational enterprise.

10. Failure to explain the high proportion of trade of developed nations that is carried on with other developed nations.
11. The reliance on general or generic factors of production and the failure to consider the unavailability of certain factors in some nations.
12. Production functions do not vary among nations.

This list of shortcomings is to be segmented. The first six items will not be directly incorporated into the core theory although reliance upon the use of money costs and prices (see 7) will permit the analyst to make allowances for such problems in instances where they assume primary importance. The generalized theory will attempt to introduce into the core theory measures that will allow the core theory to embody the dimensions cited in items 7 to 12.

1. Intranational Imperfections

This criticism of the theory was raised originally about the classical theory by John H. Williams in 1929.[9] The same concern, perhaps a legacy of Ohlin's discussions with Williams, appears in Ohlin's 'Reflections'. Williams' concern is that factors of production do not respond efficiently to differential rates of return in different areas and different industries and the economies would therefore not adapt to trade stimuli as the theory suggests. Ohlin's criticism is centred upon the locational effects of different industries; they can include possibility of the non-development of resources because of exorbitant transportation costs and upon the interrelationship between the relative facility of transportation of goods and labour in determining the interregional (intranational) pattern of output.[10] The interregional pattern of output will affect, through internal transportation costs, the money price of different commodities at national boundaries. For some products internal transportation costs can be a significant factor in f.o.b. prices.

---

[9] 'The Theory Reconsidered'.
[10] 'Reflections', paragraphs 7 and 8.

2. *The International Immobility of Factors*

This criticism of the purely classical theory is a longstanding
one. The evidence of the waves of migration from Europe to
North America, Australia and Africa offered a general refutation of the assumption. Moreover, the traffic in slaves and the
existence of sizeable international capital flows constituted
refutation of a different kind. Yet, in the timeless frame of
reference, the simplifying assumption of the international
immobility of factors of production — as a substitute for a large
differential in the case of intranational and international factor
mobility — is the only assumption that can give a precise result
(except for the less likely perfect international mobility
assumption). This problem, like that raised by the assumption
of fixed factor supplies, will yield to an analytic approach that
involves 'development through time' in which factor supplies,
and changes in factor supplies, will be determined exogenously
in successive analytic periods.[11]

3. *The Full-employment Assumption*

In the post-World War Two era, this assumption is probably not
a serious weakness when applied to analyses of the developed
world. These countries have maintained very high levels of
employment and factor—price ratios and supply factors can
probably be taken as given. Demand patterns can vary as
macro-economic policies are invoked to assure the high levels of
employment. The assumption of full employment is a more
serious weakness when applied to developing nations in which
unemployment and underemployment are widespread. In a
fully employed nation, changes in international trade patterns
will affect factor—price ratios and will affect the international
competitiveness of individual goods differently as well as having
repercussions upon demand patterns. In a country in which
excess labour exists, the factor—price ratio is not likely to be
changed as a result of an increase in export volume since there is
likely to be a perfectly elastic supply of labour to the modern
sector at some minimum or institutionally determined wage.[12]

[11] The expression is Ohlin's, see *ibid.*, p. 314.
[12] For a thorough examination of the impact of international trade and
investment upon relative factor prices in a Ranis—Fei world, see Vincent Lin, 'Trade
Preferences in the Industrial Development of Puerto Rico', unpublished PhD
dissertation, Rutgers University, 1973, ch. 4.

As a result, the increase in trade volume will be unlikely to have an important effect upon the competitiveness of different goods in international trade. The increased income, and particularly the increase in labour's share, may have significant repercussions upon the demand pattern.

Full employment is the only assumption strictly compatible with general equilibrium analysis. When the general equilibrium approach with its inherent timelessness, is discarded, it becomes possible to utilize an assumption that closely resembles full employment. Let the employable supply of labour, the feasible volume of output and the range of production possibilities of a nation be considered predetermined for a finite time period. Then, the apparatus of given demand and supply configurations can be used in a mutual interdependence price theory within that specified time period. A theory of maximal employment is to be used for poor nations.

4. *Imperfect Competition in Factor and Product Markets*

Harry G. Johnson has remarked that international trade theory has, in its central core, paid no attention to the theory of monopolistic competition.[13] While Johnson's concern is product markets for differentiated goods, the shortcoming applies as well to imperfect competition in both product and factor markets. Certainly, international trade in differentiated goods has reached such important dimensions that it can no longer reasonably be excluded from the central core theory. There is, however, some question as to whether monopoly, monopsony and similar elements need to be explicitly included in that core. In product markets, imperfections will cause relative product prices to differ from those that would exist in a perfectly competitive world. The differences will be similar to those caused by intranational transportation costs. Imperfections in factor markets will have the same general effect. What matters in international trade, and therefore in international trade theory, is the price at which a good is offered for export relative to the price at which the same (or a similar) good is available from domestic sources. The monopoly element will change relative prices and may alter the composition of internationally

[13] 'International Trade Theory and Monopolistic Competition Theory' in R. E. Kuenne, *Monopolistic Competition Theory: Studies in Impact* (New York: John Wiley and Sons, 1967), pp. 203—18.

traded goods. Imperfections in product and factor markets will also affect income distribution and could cause changes in the pattern of total demand. Provided that analyses are conducted with the pattern of demand that follows from the extant income distribution and for the product prices that actually exist, no serious consequences ensue from imperfections in domestic product and factor markets.

5. *The Effect of Social Legislation and Taxes*

The factor—proportions theory relies implicitly upon the assumption that the relative price of factors of production will be determined by their demand and supply schedules. In the modern era in which there is an abundance of social legislation designed to alter income distribution and to finance socially desirable, public-sector expenditures, relative factor prices are unlikely to reflect factor-proportions exclusively. Ohlin addresses himself to these weaknesses of the factor—proportions model and cites three important sources of discrepancies between countries in the costs of individual goods.[14] The emphasis is on the costs of goods produced as seen by corporations as opposed to the costs of factors. In this, Ohlin is, of course, perfectly correct in pointing out that in the complex modern world, multi-product firms can and must allocate overhead costs arbitrarily and may even choose to allocate them according to the buoyancy of demand for the different products. He also notes that locational problems will affect the cost of goods sold to foreigners at national frontiers. However, in his references to variation in rates of taxation upon profits, of allowed rates of depreciation, of social security taxes, Ohlin misses an opportunity to broaden the concept of the cost of factor of production. Different rates of social security or payroll taxes affect the cost of labour in the same way that heavier tax rates upon profit alter the rate of return earned by capital. In much the same way, differences in laws governing working conditions and paid vacations affect the cost of labour in different countries. However, these effects may not alter the relative costs of capital and of labour in the long run. It is

---

[14] 'The Business Cost Account Approach to International Trade Theory', loc. cit., pp. 12—20.

probably more useful to consider these items as included within the costs of capital and labour and other factors: if this is done, the price—interdependent theory of international trade will exist in near its pristine form with the only difference that relative costs of factors are the basis for international trade. Factor proportions will be a primary, though not exclusive, influence in the determination of relative factor prices.

6. International Transportation Costs

Orthodox theory has not managed to introduce the concept of transportation costs to the core theory. There are obvious difficulties — particularly in the two-good model. The crux of international trade, and trade theory, is the relative costs of a good from a domestic and from a foreign source. The cost comparison must be made at the point of use and international transportation costs can obviously play an important role in the comparison.

The complexities that derive from the very large number of goods traded by even a single nation, the alternative means and distances of transportation, the difference in the 'transportability' of different goods and the variability in the costs structures for different types of transportation, preclude any realistic integration of international transportation costs with national production costs on an aggregative basis. The best that can be said on an aggregative basis is that small differences in domestic selling prices of a good will not necessarily bring about international trade in that good. Equally, of course, factor—price equalization can never occur as a result of international trade.

On a less aggregative basis, transportation costs can be incorporated into the analysis and will have a contribution to make to any understanding of different patterns of trade in different types of goods and in individual goods. Essentially, the role of transportation costs is to affect different goods differently so that a rank ordering of goods by international competitiveness, based on domestic costs of manufacture or selling prices in the exporting country, will not be perfectly negatively correlated with a rank ordering in the importing country generated by a comparison of domestic prices with the prices of competing imports c.i.f. Presumably, such a rank ordering would rank exports at the top of the list, non-tradable goods would occupy the centre and imports would have the greatest competitive disadvantage. Goods with particularly heavy transportation costs would tend to be clustered near the centre of the list.[15]

A study of an individual commodity can reveal the effect of transportation costs on both the volume and the pattern of trade. The effect of transportations costs will, of course, feed back into the equilibrium solution through which the market-clearing rate of exchange is determined. Similarly, where groups of goods have similar characteristics, it may be possible to group them together and to allow for the importance of trans-portation costs in determining the volume and pattern of trade of that particular group. Transportation-cost characteristics can determine the distance over which goods of different types can be efficiently transported as when primary products can be transported cheaply over very long distances and enjoy cheap bulk-handling at both ends of the ocean voyage. In comparison with the low costs of ocean-borne transportation for bulk commodities such as grains, ores and oil, manufactured goods are usually transported by cargo-liner and incur much higher costs per unit of value — particularly in view of the high costs of handling at the two ports. The disparity in the transportation costs of different types of commodities can affect the terms of trade which different nations enjoy. When the commodity or net barter terms of trade are computed on the basis of imports being c.i.f. and exports f.o.b., a primary product importer will tend to have better terms of trade than an importer of finished goods, other things being equal.

A further problem that makes the integration of trans-portation costs into the core of international trade theory difficult is the structure of transportation industries themselves. Transportation industries are usually afflicted with heavy fixed costs and quite low variable costs over sizeable ranges of output. Thus, marginal cost is likely to be less than total average cost and the danger of destructive price competition exists. For this reason, most transportation industries have price schedules set by cartels or public bodies and discriminate by different classes of goods. It is difficult to combine such costs with a mutual interdependence price theory.

[15] This concept is developed in chapter 6.

7. *The Failure to Incorporate Money Costs and Prices*

Criticism of the reliance of classical theory on real costs was an important feature of Ohlin's original treatise. Ohlin stressed the necessity for a mutual interdependence *price* theory and the essential role of prices: 'The immediate cause of trade is always that goods can be bought cheaper from outside in terms of money than they can be produced at home and vice versa'.[16] However, by showing little interest in working with the more complex version of his model, he set a precedent in the reliance upon the simple formal model and pointed the way toward what now reigns as orthodoxy.[17] The decision variable in the two-factor, two-good model is relative factor prices. Since only two factors are involved, this ratio does not have to be expressed in terms of money prices at all and the price level and the rate of exchange are not features of the usual version of the orthodox theory. Where multiple goods are involved in the model, but still only two factors, the concept of a critical borderline good has proved useful in separating imports from exports and, naturally, the factor-intensity of the borderline good determines the dividing line without recourse to money prices.[18]

The introduction of multiple factors of production — not all of which are used in each good — reduces the usefulness of a unit of an input as the numeraire and makes the strong factor-intensity assumption worthless. When more than two factors of production are used, the use of domestic currency as a numeraire and the definition of prices and costs in that numeraire becomes a more reliable approach. The use of domestic currencies also requires that international price comparisons be made through a rate of exchange between the two numeraires and, in this way, the theory becomes more realistic and more easily related to balance-of-payments theory.

There is an additional advantage to defining prices in money terms. Five of the six shortcomings of the orthodox theory discussed to this point, involve the possibility of differences between the actual and the 'ideal' set of prices. The ideal set of

[16] *Interregional and International Trade* (1933), pp. 12–13.

[17] Caves, *Trade and Economic Structure*, p. 27.

[18] See, for example, Paul A. Samuelson, 'Theoretical Notes on Trade Problems,' *The Review of Economics and Statistics*, XLVI (May 1964) p. 146, but see Bhagwati, 'The Heckscher–Ohlin Theorem in the Multi-Commodity Case,' *op. cit.*, for a qualification.

prices is that which would be generated in a perfectly competitive economy with zero transportation costs and no tax and expenditure problem. In such an ideal economy, factor proportions, together with demand and production functions, would determine the relative prices of goods in different countries before and after trade was established. The five shortcomings (1 and 3 to 6)[19] involve variation between the *cost of a factor* under real-world and ideal conditions (3, 4, and 5), between the *cost of a product* under real-world and ideal conditions (1 and 6), and between the *price* of the product under the two sets of conditions (4). Thus, one of the major criticisms of the orthodox model is that it derives relative prices too easily. By the same token, however, if prices are deemed to be generated by a more complex procedure, these prices could be inserted into a model and used to explain the trade patterns that occur.

The validity of these critiques is not subject to dispute. What is debatable is whether these points could usefully be integrated into the central or core theory of international trade. The most important determinant of the prices of individual goods is the cost of production and, therefore, of input costs. For particular studies of the influence of international trade upon different industries, the core theory may well be developed to reduce any inaccuracies that obtain from a straightforward reliance upon factor proportions as the basis for relative prices. It does not follow from that that these phenomena warrant inclusion in the core theory itself. The underlying cause of international trade and the repercussions of the existence of international trade on the economies concerned are closely linked with factor proportions. It is by means of change in the demand-supply configurations for different factors of production that international trade exerts its influence upon costs structures of different goods, income distribution and, through that, upon demand patterns. Moreover, given the existing set of imperfections in goods and factor markets, changes in international trade patterns will work their effects through changes in relative factor prices. Thus, while the factor proportions model needs

---

[19] The question of international factor mobility is best handled separately in a 'development through time' model, but it could be incorporated in this general area of variation between ideal and actual as a cause of variation in factor pricing.

qualifying for these phenomena in a static sense, it will still provide a good basis for analysis of reaction to *change* in demand patterns or factor endowments. Of course, changes in market structure and changes affecting factor and product prices can come about independently of international trade factors. In this case, the analysis will have to allow for them quite explicitly. Equally, it is important to recognize that changes in market structure brought about by international trade could have a secondary effect upon the final pattern of trade. In the same way, attempts to offset the impact of international forces on domestic income distribution will have a secondary effect. Neither of these phenomena is likely to be of first-order magnitude that will warrant inclusion in the core theory.

The preservation of a manageability in the core theory is vital. The criticisms apply, importantly, only to specialized analyses. They are, then, explicit warning to theorists using the core theory for particular purposes, that the intent of the analysis and the core theory may be incompatible. The theory offered in chapters 4 and 5 will not attempt to incorporate these effects directly. However, in so far as that theory avoids the timelessness of general equilibrium, it will be possible to incorporate known changes in factor or product prices deliberately — by hand, as it were. It is the aim of the generalized theory to embody the dimensions of shortcomings 7 to 12 and, by doing so, to widen the analytic range of the framework.

8.   *Linear Homogeneous Production Functions*

Formalized models of the orthodox variety almost invariably rely on the qualities of production functions of this type.[20] In the real world, returns to scale are not constant over wide ranges of output and it is possible for scale variables alone to make any production of a good in a country inefficient despite the availability of all necessary inputs. While economies of scale normally accrue to producers in large rich nations with large domestic markets, exports can also serve as a means of achieving

---

[20] Caves in *Trade and Economic Structure*, p. 74, is resigned to this excessive simplification. Hufbauer in *Synthetic Materials and the Theory of International Trade* explicitly introduces what he calls the scale economy account.

economies of scale and will enable production units in small countries to be internationally competitive. Reliance upon exports for the achievement of scale economies can be dangerous unless the country has a long-run comparative advantage in the good concerned and if the export market is likely to be susceptible to foreign commercial policy measures. The distinction is also drawn between economies of scale of the kind described above and the dynamic economies of scale that involve cost reductions through learning. To include the cost effects of learning in a theory of international trade requires that the volume of past production be included in the production function and that the theory achieve some escape from the timelessness that characterizes the general equilibrium model.[21]

9. Emphasis on Finished Goods

It is not possible in a two-good model to consider intermediate products. When the number of goods is increased, the introduction of intermediate goods can be accomplished to a limited degree in the orthodox two-factor analysis but the result is hardly 'useful'.[22] At any point in time, the global matrix of comparative advantage is influenced by the historic international mobility of basic factors of production (physical capital, labour, human capital and knowledge) since existing factor endowments depend upon these movements. Additionally, the matrix is affected by the ability of intermediate products to move internationally since, if a nation can import an input more cheaply than it can obtain that input from domestic sources, the nation's competitiveness in the market for the final good is improved. The distinction between the two types of input is worth making because basic factors of production move in response to different forces than do primary or intermediate products. The difference between the flows of the two types of input is partly dependent upon the

[21] See Hufbauer, *op. cit.*, pp. 21–23 and M. V. Posner's seminal article, 'international Trade and Technical Change,' *Oxford Economic Papers* (October 1961) pp. 323–41.

[22] R. N. Batra and F. R. Casas, 'Intermediate Products and the Pure Theory of International Trade: A Neo-Heckscher–Ohlin Framework,' *American Economic Review* LXIII (June 1973), pp. 297–311.

reversibility of the flow and partly upon the speed with which the flow can be generated. Both types of input respond to the costs of transfer and for trade in or movement of inputs to be instigated, the benefits must exceed the costs of transfer.

Costs of transfer include transportation costs, information costs, risk exposure and the cost of impediments to transfer. The costs of impediments to transfer may be absolute when immigration laws prevent labour migration, when direct investments are prohibited by host governments or when a tariff on an intermediate product is prohibitive. Risk will deter the transfer of physical capital, labour and knowledge. Information costs will, like transportation costs, vary widely among products. Transportation costs are obvious factors affecting the efficient location of intermediate production processes when primary products are to be used in finished goods in a country other than those in which the primary product is produced.[23] International movement of factors of production will take place when the costs of transfer are outweighed by the private (and efficiency) gains that will accrue from movement. International trade in intermediate products takes place when the costs of transfer are not large enough to counter differences in costs of production in different nations.

It is impossible to separate international movements of inputs from the existence of international and multinational enterprise. This organizational form can reduce information costs, achieve economies of scale — in transportation costs as well as in production —[24], and can bring about the movements of basic factors of production on a temporary arrangement as well as permanently. Multi-national enterprise can contrast the costs of production in different nations under varying rates of output with the transfer costs that will be incurred by each alternative combination of inputs and locational distribution.

Any theory of international trade must be able to encompass the existence of multi-national enterprises. The theory must be able to explain both the pattern of trade that exists in inputs and outputs at any given time and the factors that lead to a

---

[23] The best succinct discussion of all these aspects is in Robert E. Baldwin, 'International Trade in Inputs and Outputs,' *American Economic Review* LX (May 1970), pp. 430–34. The location question is essentially that of 'footloose' industries examined by Hufbauer in *Synthetic Materials and the Theory of International Trade.*

[24] See John H. Dunning, 'The Determinants of International Production,' *op. cit.*

change in that pattern of trade in inputs, the pattern of resource endowments and the repercussions upon the pattern of trade in outputs.

10. Failure to Explain the High Proportion of International Trade Carried on among Rich Nations

The orthodox theory would lead the analyst to expect that the greater volume of international trade would take place between groups of nations that have significant differences in their factor endowments — presumably between those nations with surplus labour and those with proportionately large stocks of capital. Empirically, this is not borne out for trade in manufactures — that category of international trade that best fits the orthodox theory. The major critic of this inapplicability of orthodoxy is S. B. Linder. His counter-theory explains a high proportionate volume of trade between nations with similar endowments.[25] Linder emphasizes two characteristics of modern economies: a domestic market is a prerequisite for a domestic productive unit to be able to achieve the economies of scale for international viability; and that nations with similar income levels have similar tastes in so far as the type of goods and the sophistication of those goods are concerned. Similarity of tastes enhances the number of commodities produced domestically that are potential exports and the number of foreign commodities that are potential imports. Therefore, the closer the levels of national income, the greater is the potential volume of international trade between two countries likely to be. Trade may take place in both directions in differentiated, monopolistically competitive goods between nations with very similar resource endowments. Potential trade in manufactures between pairs of nations with similar incomes will be high but there is little likelihood of much trade in manufactures between a poor, labour-surplus country and a rich country because of the small overlap in demand for the 'quality' of manufactured goods produced in the two countries. These factors determine the amount of potential trade. The volume of trade that actually

[25] Staffan Burenstam Linder, *An Essay on Trade and Transformation* (Stockholm: Almqvist and Wiksell, 1961), especially pp. 87–109; reprinted in part in Robert E. Baldwin and J. David Richardson, *International Trade and Finance: Readings* (Boston: Little, Brown and Company, 1974), pp. 43–54.

takes place will depend closely upon the volume of potential trade and the degree to which this trade is impeded by 'trade-braking' forces such as tariffs, transportation costs and non-tariff barriers.

Linder's counter-theory supports the observed, rapid increase in two-way or intra-industry trade observed within the European Economic Community when tariffs among members were reduced.[26]

11. The Reliance upon Generic Factors of Production

The orthodox theory of international trade labours under a paradox. Its emphasis on the generic factors of capital and labour,[27] causes the theory to exclude in advance those groups of factors in which differences in resource endowment are absolute — climate, mineral deposits among other things. Second, the theory rests heavily on two generic factors both of which are capable of movement across boundaries. Third, the emphasis on generic factors eliminates from consideration the subtleties of differences in quality of factors to the great detriment of its empirical value. The last aspect has been borne out beyond any doubt by the success of adding human capital to the two generic factors as an underlying cause of international trade.[28] In this context, it is worth noting that there has been, recently, one highly innovative attempt to develop a theory of international trade that would rid the traditional theory of some of its more glaring weaknesses.[29] Kenen's attempt to treat capital as a co-operative factor of production appeals to common sense and would allow for human and real

[26] See Bela Balassa, 'Tariff Reductions and Trade in Manufactures Among the Industrial Countries,' *American Economic Review* LVI (June 1966) pp. 466—73 and Herbert G. Grubel, 'Intra-Industry Specialization and the Pattern of Trade,' *The Canadian Journal of Economics and Political Science* 33 (August 1967), pp. 374—88.

[27] For a discussion of the implications of generic factors, see Roy Harrod, 'Factor-Price Relations under Free Trade,' *Economic Journal* LXVIII (June 1958), pp. 245—47. Harrod asserts that the use of generic factors has 'shunted the theory of international values on to the wrong track.'

[28] See, *inter alia*, W. W. Leontief, 'Factor Proportions and the Structure of American Trade: Further Theoretical and Empirical Analysis,' *Review of Economics and Statistics* XXXVIII (November 1956), pp. 386—407 and the work of Donald B. Keesing in Peter B. Kenen and Roger Lawrence (eds.) *The Open Economy* (New York: Columbia University Press, 1968).

[29] Peter B. Kenen, 'Nature, Capital and Trade,' *Journal of Political Economy* 73 (October 1965), pp. 437—60.

capital to be divided according to some rational criterion. In this way, Kenen attempted to save the factor–proportions approach and the orthodox version of international trade theory. Highly innovative though this approach may have been, it retained one of the central weaknesses of the traditional model in that it tacitly assumed that all (both) goods were capable of being produced in all (both) countries from universally available factors of production.

Another alternative to the traditional theory which discards the concept of generic and universally available factors of production has been evolved by Kravis.[30] This theory emphasizes that trade takes place to an important degree, in goods which are not available from domestic sources. This inability to produce at home may stem from the lack of a specific input – a natural resource –, technical change and product differentiation (or, presumably, innovation) which confers an absolute monopoly on the innovating country.[31] A fourth category could be the existence of limited natural resources in one country that makes imports a necessity given the level of domestic demand at the going import price. In his celebrated empirical test of the orthodox theory, Leontief correctly excluded from his analysis, goods which could not be produced in the United States. In his second article, he also excluded goods which had inelastic supply so that incremental imports were not competitive with additional domestic production and, by doing so, resolved the paradox.[32] It is obvious that disregard of international trade in non-competitive goods is a severe limitation of the orthodox model if only because of the large volume of international trade conducted in this type of good. This phenomenon is part and parcel of the process that led the orthodox model away from Heckscher and his emphasis upon many categories of factors in the factor–proportions

---

[30] I. B. Kravis, 'Availability and Other Influences on the Composition of Trade,' *Journal of Political Economy* 64 (April 1956), pp. 143–55.

[31] Jagdish Bhagwati, 'The Pure Theory of International Trade: A Survey,' *Economic Journal* LXXIV (March 1964), pp. 1–84 gives a good summary of Kravis' argument and some insightful extensions.

[32] Wassily Leontief, 'Domestic Production and Foreign Trade; the American Capital Position Re-examined,' in R. E. Caves and H. G. Johnson (eds.), *Readings in International Economics* (Homewood, Ill.: Richard D. Irwin, 1968), pp. 503–27; and W. W. Leontief, 'Factor Proportions and the Structure of American Trade,' *op. cit.*, pp. 395–98 (computation D).

model. Disregard of non-competitive goods must also invalidate deductions about income distribution both within and between trading nations since the returns to scarce resources for which no substitutions can be made generates a rent that can be paid internationally as well as intranationally. The omission of specific factors is tantamount to inserting some zero elements in the complex matrix that underlies international trade.[33]

The fact that the lack of a specific factor of production in a nation is an obvious cause of international trade does not mean that the consequent flow of trade is either negligible or uninteresting. The arrant neglect of non-competitive trade probably stems from the emphasis on the two-good model and from the superiority of comparative advantage over absolute advantage as a basis for international trade theory. What was lost sight of in the process of the development of the theory of comparative advantage, is that absolute advantage is a special case of comparative advantage. The de-emphasis of trade in non-competitive goods should, therefore, not have happened.

12. *Production Functions do not Vary Among Nations*

While aspects of this criticism of orthodox trade theory have been touched upon in some of the points made previously, this question of the identity of production functions in different nations is of paramount importance in its own right. Ignoring scale economies and limited supplies of specific factors, the identity of production functions is fundamental to the ortho-dox theory and therefore to derivative theories such as factor price equalization. It is, too, the crucial difference between the factor—proportions theory and the classical theory. In the Heckscher version of the factor—proportions theory, all known factors (including qualitative differences in similar factors) were variable within the individual functions. In this way, Heck-scher's working assumption that the techniques of production would be the same in different countries, is not a serious constraint. In the strictest of all classical formulations, the production function absorbed all variation in production other

---

[33] Ohlin is particularly concerned with this criticism in 'Reflections' pp. 309—11. See also Ohlin, 'The Business Cost Approach,' *op. cit.*, p. 13.

than that of labour's output. Thus if a production function is written as:

$$Q = f(X_1, X_2, X_3, \ldots, X_n)$$

where the X_i are inputs, the question of the identity of production functions revolves around the negative relationship between the variability of f and the size of n. The larger is n, the more easily can f be considered as identical among nations. But there is a serious question as to whether, from an operational point of view, n can ever be sufficiently large since production functions will reflect elements other than economic relationhips and physical laws.

Ohlin was the first, in 1933, to specify rigorously that the production function for a good should be considered identical in all nations. His reasoning was progressing on literary lines and was more in conformity with Heckscher's approach than with the two-factor, Casselian formulation. Ohlin asserted that 'the physical conditions of production were everywhere the same'.[34] Three things made this assertion necessary for the factor—proportions theory: the timelessness of the model precluded the possibility that production functions would be different or would require that that difference would be maintained unchanged through time; the assertion was necessary for the total emphasis on the all-important·role of factor proportions; the assertion is valid in so far as it derives, as Ohlin derives it, from the laws of natural science rather than from the behaviour of economic systems.[35] Once the assertion was linked with the two-factor version of the Casselian approach, the orthodox theory of international trade was pointed down the primrose path of analytic dalliance. Ohlin did mention the possibility of dropping the assumption but showed no interest in working with such a system in his original work.[36]

Later, in 'Reflections', Ohlin was more aware of the dangers inherent in the assumption of identical production functions.

---

[34] *Interregional and International Trade* (1933), p. 15.

[35] *Ibid.*, p. 14.

[36] See Caves, *Trade and Economic Structure*, p. 27. This whole discussion should be qualified by pointing out that the orthodox theory can incorporate production functions that are Hicks-neutrally different.

This awareness seems to stem from the overly precise theorems that depended upon the assumption. In his supportive statement, he falls back upon the multi-factor approach: 'An assumption of differing production functions is superfluous because the complete absence of certain kinds of labour or natural resources has the same effect as if their prices were so high that demand was zero'; and on an admitted panacea: 'The differing quality of managerial labour between countries is a kind of *deus ex machina*, which takes care of most of the difficulties that do not properly fit into the simple frame-work'.[37] But, immediately after these contentions, Ohlin considers seriously the risks involved in the assumption and nowhere in 'Reflections' does he endorse the two-factor approach.

There is an argument for specifying differences in production functions that derive from the general character of the two economies. In this argument, the non-economic and non-physical characteristics of the nations would qualify a production function. Such characteristics might include the distribution of human skills among the population (as opposed to reliance upon the ratio of the stock of human capital to the population or to the work force), the energy of the labour force, the knowhow and aggressiveness of management, the degree of vertical social mobility, the efficiency of the network of communications and other infrastructural features of the nation. Additionally, the social and political structures are themselves likely to be important determinants of production. Not all these features are exactly non-economic but they do lend themselves better to modifiers of a production function than to an element in it and can usefully be subsumed under the broad rubric of societal factors.

The importance of managerial differences can serve as a case in point — if only because Ohlin would use it as an element in the function. Managerial technology differs from other inputs in that it has as a basis a costless factor such as the accepted pattern of behaviour — it is societal in origin to a large degree. Further, it can undergo changes without significant opportunity costs. Differences in managerial technology are to be seen

---

[37] Pp. 310–11.

separately from human capital because they do not require abstinence from consumption or other forms of capital formation to generate changes in managerial standards. Gains from managerial efficiency will be spread unevenly across the range of products and affect relative costs differently and through that, the pattern of trade.[38]

Thus, it is reasonable to argue, with classical theorists, that production functions are not everywhere the same even though the properties of the physical world may be. Superimposed upon natural laws and economic forces are societal—attitudinal traits that affect the efficiency of production. However, it is also reasonable to argue with the factor—proportions adherents that, provided an adequate number of economic variables is included in the production function and if the social structure of two nations are the same (or very similar), then the identity of production functions is an operational simplification.[39] This approach will be most important for analyses of trade between developed and less-developed nations since production functions will be most disparate between rich and poor countries.

CONCLUSION

This chapter has identified a model of international trade theory that can be considered to represent an extreme version of orthodoxy. The major criticisms of the body of trade theory have been reviewed. Some of the criticisms of the body of theory were deemed to be of insufficient general importance to warrant their inclusion in a core theory of international trade. Other criticisms, the reliance upon linear, homogeneous production functions that do not differ among nations, the failure to consider trade in inputs, the failure to include factors that need not be available in all nations, were deemed important enough to warrant integration in a pragmatic core theory. What the generalized theory is attempting to achieve is then, to

[38] The whole question of managerial efficiency recalls Leontief's explanation of his paradox, Mr. W. Mansfield-Williams provided valuable insights on the societal—attitudinal aspects of managerial efficiency.

[39] National income *per capita* may prove to be a good measure of the quality of the infrastructure and therefore will constitute a first measure of the similarity or lack of similarity that may be expected of production functions in two countries.

establish some commonality of ground between the usefulness of the factor—proportions theory as a means of interrelating trade and its domestic repercussions in a mutual price interdependent system, with those factors that rob the orthodox version of its underlying strength.

3 The Concepts Underlying the Generalized Theory

The purpose of this chapter is to introduce the three concepts that broaden the traditional model and allow it to apply to a wider range of real-world problems. The three concepts are interrelated. Consequently, the order of their introduction is determined by expositional considerations rather than by any measure of the importance of the concepts. The three concepts are: an explicit time dimension; a three-part production function; and the integration into the model of three different types of goods.

THE TIME DIMENSION

One of the shortcomings of the orthodox theory of international trade, as well as of the classical theory, is its inability to incorporate the passage of time. Attempts to dynamize the model either involve growth models in which, usually, the supply of one or more factors increases at a constant (absolute) rate or at some steady rate of growth, or they involve exercises in comparative statics in which the exogenous change in the model need not be dictated by the theory but can be arrived at haphazardly.

The characteristic of timelessness is one of the main reasons that the orthodox version cannot usefully adapt itself to several real-world phenomena. These phenomena include the international transfer of technology, of physical and human capital, and of labour. The basic cause lies in the identity of production functions in both (all) countries. A theory that excludes time from its domain, cannot logically specify a difference between production functions in two nations unless it is willing to countenance that degree of difference existing in perpetuity. It is more convincing to argue that, because the physical laws of production are everywhere the same, production functions must be the same in all nations than to argue the existence in one country of an ability to use knowledge that is 'in the public domain' being greater than that ability in the second nation *and* that this difference in ability will endure indefinitely. An alternative to ability to use public knowledge is the unequal availability of proprietary knowledge that because of its inherent characteristics cannot provide a constant advantage to one nation over time. Finally, the timelessness of the orthodox model is one of the obstacles to the introduction into the analysis of differentiated goods whose features and design, and therefore their competitive advantage, change on a regular basis.

A finite time dimension is essential if the generalized theory is to incorporate the international transfer of factors of production. Flow analysis cannot incorporate factor movements in an equilibrium model without introducing quite arbitrary and restrictive constraints upon the stock situation. The most obvious case in point is the increase in transfer payments by the nation receiving technology and/or capital. Transfer payments will affect the competitiveness of the two nations and will confound any model based on timeless equilibrium. The existence of a finite time dimension also facilitates the incorporation into the core theory of changes in factor supplies internal to the nations, changes in product design that affect the market for differentiated goods in foreign countries and the evolution of modifiers to the production functions. The existence of a finite time dimension prepares the analyst for successive real disturbances (changes in data) that the real world generates at irregular intervals. Timeless models tend to pre-dispose the analyst to consideration of a world in which real disturbances come singly and infrequently enough for the system to establish a new equilibrium. This distinction borders upon the question of the philosophy of the theorist and upon his view of the world. While it may be possible to evolve dynamic systems with disequilibrium, it is unlikely that such systems would also be able to incorporate the other dimensions to be developed in this chapter without exceeding the allowable degree of complexity. The most suitable, though by no means perfect vehicle for introducing the time dimension is a variation of period analysis.

Period Analysis

Period analysis has been defined as the 'splitting of time into periods such that, apart from exogenous changes, the events of any period can be explained with reference to previous periods'.[1] The hallmark of period analysis is its discontinuity. It evolves the expectation that change in the underlying conditions will occur at frequent, regular intervals. These changes can be of two kinds: those which are purely exogenous and those which are induced from the evolution of the system in previous periods. The great advantage of period analysis for pragmatic theorizing is that it imposes upon the investigator a mental cast that is keyed to dynamic disturbance.

Period analysis cannot avoid making simplifications that constrain real-world conditions into artificiality. Period analysis works in a sequence of period, 'shift', period and a never-ending series of alternating shifts and periods thereafter. Within the period, adjustment towards equilibrium takes place. There is no assurance that equilibrium will be reached. The actual attainment of equlibrium will depend upon the speed of reaction of the system and upon the length of the period. However, it is assumed that all variables adjust from their values at the beginning *toward* their ultimate equilibrium values.[2] A shift is that moment between periods when all disturbances actually take place. The exogenous disturbances occur simultaneously with the induced disturbances. Exogenous disturbances need no comment. Induced disturbances are those changes in the global distribution of factors of production that occur as a result of adjustments in preceding periods. For example, the process of adjustment may have so raised the potential return to a piece of proprietary technological knowhow in the country that lacks it, that the transfer of knowhow becomes attractive; or a new pattern of factor allocation may have increased the return to labour to a degree sufficient to overcome any obstacles to in-migration that may exist.

---

[1] The best treatment of period analysis and the source of the quotations are William J. Baumol, (with a contribution by Ralph Turvey), *Economic Dynamics: An Introduction*, 2nd ed. (New York: The Macmillan Company, 1959), ch. 8.

[2] When the changes that occur during a shift are very severe, the system may be unstable (recede away from ultimate equilibrium) during one or two periods. The question of possible instability is not considered here.

Of all the constraints exerted upon reality by period analysis, the length of the period is the most important. In its original form, period analysis is oriented towards macro-economics and is concerned with decision periods and the reconciliation of *ex ante* intentions and *ex post* achievements. The length of the period is arbitrary; the shorter the period, the less is the strain imposed upon the system by forcing the timing of disturbances into simultaneity, but the less is the progress toward equilibrium made in any one period. When time series work is based upon period analysis, the form in which the data are available frequently dictates the length of the period and overrides conceptual niceties.

The generalized theory will incorporate a variant form of period analysis that is deemed to be better suited than the original version to clarifying the theory of international trade. The variant is a simplified version of the original and its adoption does not, in any way, preclude the use of the traditional form of period analysis in the generalized theory. The crux of the difference is the assumption about the progress made toward equilibrium in a single period. In the variant version, the length of the period is the time needed for an economy fully to adapt to a change in its factor endowment or in its production function in the preceding shift.[3] Thus, within a period, t, product and factor prices will change so that the output-mix, the consumption-mix and the volume and composition of trade will have attained a short-run equilibrium. (The time interval is clearly analogous to Marshall's short period.) However, factor prices can be such that the ensuing shift between periods, $t+$, will bring forth increments to (decrements from) domestic factor supplies as well as instigating the international movement of any of the mobile factors of production. For example, if a piece of technological knowhow were to be transferred in $t-$, the length of the ensuing period, t, is that in which the technological innovation is ingested into the recipient economy so that it will produce a new set of factor prices given the inability of the quantity of a factor supplied to change within a period.

---

[3] Periods are numbered $t-1$, t, $t+1$ as usual. Shifts are numbered $t-1-$, $t-$, $t+$, $t+1+$. Clearly, shift $t-$ could also be numbered $t-1+$ but shifts are numbered 'outward' from period t.

The expositional advantages provided by the variant form of period analysis are offset to some degree by the significant degree of artificiality that the methodology imposes upon the theory. The period must be constant from period to period. All disturbances must therefore be ingested into the recipient economy within the specified length of time. Thus, there is an implicit suggestion that the length of time needed for the ingestion of a disturbance is independent of the kind of disturbance — a technological change taking as long to be adapted to as will a change in the supply of capital of labour. Equally, for any given set of speeds of ingestion, there is a maximum disturbance with which the analytic system can cope. This artificiality is less constraining in orthodox period analysis since orthodox period analysis allows for the possibility of truncated adjustment to a disturbance within the ensuing period and for further adjustments in following periods.

The advantages of the short-run period are that it permits the theory to ascribe changes in the volume and pattern of trade and in factor and product prices to be unequivocally related to the events of the preceding shift. In the same way, it is possible to attribute events occurring within a shift, $t+$, either to changes in factor prices between t and $t-1$ or to outside events. There is no hangover of distributed-lag effects from $t-1$ so that changes in period t or in shift $t+$ may derive either from delayed reactions to earlier phenomena or from changes in the preceding element in the sequence. The full assumptions are, necessarily, quite heroic but they become less stringent when the theory is applied to a particular phenomenon or a single disturbance. The assumptions are: (1) a period is long enough to allow full adjustment to the set of data that existed at the beginning of the period; (2) all countries have the same length of period and the period does not vary irrespective of the magnitude of the disturbance experienced in the preceding shift; and (3) all changes in data occur instantaneously between periods and there is no decision lag so that any changes in factor supplies in $t+1$ brought about by the new factor prices generated in t take place simultaneously in $t+$.

Using this treatment of the time dimension, it will be possible for resource endowments, tastes and production functions to change at regular intervals within the analytic framework.

THE THREE-PART PRODUCTION FUNCTION

While the orthodox theory does not neglect the influence of demand factors on the final pattern of trade, the pattern of demand derives from a set of tastes that are not generated within the model itself. This set of tastes will change in response to changes in the level of income and, ostensibly, in the distribution of that income but these are the only aspects of demand that are integrated into the analytic framework. Given the relatively superficial analysis of demand factors, the emphasis of international trade theory must be on supply factors. Central to questions of supply are the resource endowments of the nations and the production functions of the individual goods. For this reason, the restrictions placed upon the production function in the orthodox theory are crucial.

The generalized theory requires that production functions be able to differ among nations and through time as a part of the logical sequence. Such a production function must have three separate components: an input-mix element; a 'modifier'; and a 'scalar'; Given the money prices of inputs, the production function will determine the cost functions of individual goods and, except for differentiated goods, marginal cost pricing is assumed to hold.[4] Factor prices are determined by their marginal revenue products.[5] Thus the model is a price-independent theory in which all markets are in short-run flow equilibrium at the end of each period.

The input-mix element is the familiar and standard part of the production function. It expresses the functional relationship between the mix and quantity of inputs and the quantity of outputs. Indirectly the input-mix specifies the marginal physical product of each factor and, given factor prices, allows the minimum cost mix to be computed. Substitution among inputs is assumed possible on a continuously differentiable basis and is subject to diminishing marginal rates of substitution.

The input-mix for a single good can then be written:

$$Q_1 = f_1(X_1, X_2, X_3, \ldots, X_n) \tag{3-1}$$

[4] The pricing of differentiated goods is developed below. For the rationale of marginal cost pricing, see p. 22 above.

[5] When natural resources of varying quality are introduced, there is a problem in defining the unit of input (see below in this chapter). For the rationale for the assumption of perfect factor markets see pp. 17 and 18 above.

The immediate problem for the construction of a core theory of international trade is whether or not n should be constrained and, if so, at what number. The purely unconstrained version would comply with Heckscher's original conception of the factor — proportions theory. Setting n equal to 2 with the two inputs being capital and labour would accord with the orthodox theory.

Modern research has evolved five main categories of inputs that will affect the production of a good in such a way that the role of national resource endowments will be clearly seen. These inputs are: physical capital (K), labour (L), human capital (H), natural resources (R), and proprietary knowledge belonging to individuals or firms (P). The input-mix for good 1 is then:

$$Q_1 = f_1(K, L, H, R, P) \qquad (3\text{-}2)$$

Labour and capital are inevitable and traditional and need no explanation. Labour itself is unimproved and is improved by human capital which represents the availability of skills in the work force.[6] Natural resources can include mineral deposits, types of land and climate. Essentially, the input R is the only one that is not capable of international migration. The fifth variable, proprietary knowledge, is not universally accessible except through the permission of its owners. This type of knowledge comprises many sorts of knowhow, usually the fruit of experience in the owners' own national market or of research and investment outlays, which are not in the public domain. Proprietary knowledge can be contrasted with the more basic knowledge which is generally known and can be obtained by any firm or nation without cost. Proprietary knowledge can be obtained by a nation through a licensing agreement or by having the foreign owners of the knowledge invest in production within its boundaries.[7] Of course, proprietary knowledge cannot be held unchanging in a timeless state. The essence of the role of P in the structure of international trade is that the amount available in any country can change over time both in

---

[6] This follows from Kenen, 'Nature, Capital and Trade'.

[7] The concept of private knowledge as a public good is developed in H. G. Johnson, 'The Efficiency and Welfare Implications of the International Corporation', in C. P. Kindleberger (ed.), *The International Corporation*, (Cambridge: M.I.T. Press, 1970), ch. 2.

particular industries and in the aggregate as P seeps from the private to the public domain.

While the physical conditions of production and the availability of basic scientific knowledge are indeed everywhere the same, the ability to make use of that basic knowledge may be modified or affected by the characteristics of the focus economy and may differ from nation to nation. This possibility requires that the production function contain a modifying element that will alter the input-mix element to take cognizance of the limited ability of some countries to take advantage of basic knowledge. The modifier will vary from nation to nation and must, therefore, be identified by the nation. In most instances in which the pattern of trade of a single nation vis-a-vis the rest of the world is concerned, the modifier will denote a difference in the ability of the focus nation to use basic knowledge in the production of a good in comparison with the most efficient foreign producer. Thus, modifiers will seldom appear in analyses of developed-manufacturing nations but they will appear quite frequently in analyses of developing nations' trade patterns. There are two ways in which a limited ability to make use of the basic knowledge available in the world can affect the ability to produce a good. First, the limitation may derive from the lack of a suitable resource base when some resources were very scarce and enjoyed opportunity costs too high to enable them to be used in certain industries and, therefore, to enable that industry to make use of all the knowledge potentially available. Such a phenomenon would be registered in the input-mix and not in the modifier element of the production function.[8]

But a restricted ability to use basic knowledge may also derive from the general characteristics of the economy of the society and, in this case, the production function for a good would need modification. A nation's socio-economic structure may not endow it with the ability to embody the total stock of available technology into its productive sector. There are several factors which are likely to affect the ability to embody basic knowledge and these will exert their effect upon the input-mix element by means of a modifier. Primarily, the factors are societal and attitudinal. They can include political

[8] Cf. Ohlin in 'Reflections', p. 310.

constraints on resource allocation and trade such as might occur in a nation that severely constrains its domestic resource allocation to conform with either *bona fide* national goals or avowed ideologies. The aggressiveness and professional standards of the managerial class, probably largely determined by peer group pressure and social standards, and the energy and sense of dedication of the workers will both severely modify any production function. The attitudinal flexibility of entrepreneurs and residents, the generality of taboos and the conservatism of the peasantry will all affect the degree to which modern knowhow can be incorporated into the productive sector. The intranational mobility of factors of productions, the efficiency of local capital markets, the distribution of human capital among the work force and the general level of infrastructure can all affect the degree to which the socio-economic characteristics of a nation can affect the degree to which basic knowledge can be applied. An example of how this can affect its output capability can be seen with the irrationality of producing computers in India. There, the lack of a sufficiently integrated industrial sector, the general weakness of the work force in quality control and the relatively poor quality of the communications network makes the production of a highly complex and sophisticated good impracticable in the sense that the unsuitability of the economy prevents computers being made at anything approaching reasonable costs. This, of course, does not mean that India is incapable of producing computers if opportunity costs were to be disregarded.

The modifiers will apply unequally to different goods and will affect the efficiency of individual inputs differently. Thus, the modifier is not multiplicative for each element inside the input-mix element affecting the efficiency of each element equally in the way in which neutral technical change is incorporated into some of the more modern theoretical models. The input-mix elements are similar to the production functions of Ohlin. In the absence of modifiers, the input-mix elements are determined by the 'physical conditions of production' — that is by the available basic knowledge. These are the same for all nations. Thus, for identical national modifiers, the production functions will be identical in all nations. To the extent that the ability to use basic knowledge is likely to be positively correlated with the stage of development and the level of *per capita* income, the modifiers will be more important in the analysis of the trade patterns of developing nations. In the same way, imperfections in the socio-economic characteristics of a nation (measured against some perfectly efficient economic state) will also be more important in developing economies and will require a distinctive modifier. But nations that suffer from deep-seated political antagonisms and consequent economic inefficiency will also require modifiers even though the nations be generally considered as 'advanced'. Great Britain and Italy are cases in point in the mid-seventies. In such nations, the modifiers will vary by sector and by industry if certain industries are more seriously affected by the political antagonisms than other. In Great Britain the automotive industry would require its own modifier because of the problems of labour—management relations and production and marketing weaknesses.

The orthodox theory has been considered to be more likely to apply to trade between a bloc of developed nations and a bloc of poorer nations. This contention springs directly from the Ohlin model and, more particularly, from Linder's distinction between the causes of trade in primary goods and manufactured goods.[9] The existence of modifiers will be likely to accentuate this applicability of the factor—proportions theory to trade between blocs of nations of unequal development. No nation can have a comparative advantage in all goods and, where a nation's production functions for different goods are affected by modifiers, those goods with the greatest favourable modifications or least unfavourable modification (relative to competitors') will be more likely to be exported.

The imposition of constant returns to scale on production functions by the orthodox theory was a theorist's simplification. It was an unfortunate innovation. In fact, economics of large-scale production are achieved by firms in almost every industry or endeavour. Scale economies are achieved in transportation, and marketing as well as in production and can preclude the manufacture of a particular good in a country. Simply because of the inability of firms in a country to achieve the cost-reductions available to its foreign competition, a nation may not be able to produce a certain good despite enjoying a comparative advantage in that good when costs were based solely on production functions and inputs prices. This set of

[9] See point 10 in chapter 2, p. 26.

circumstances, if the nation is large enough to demand the output of a competitively sized firm, is one of the bases for infant industry protection.

Scale economies can affect the global distribution of production and the pattern of trade. The scale advantages accrue to firms that are the first to develop a product since the lead provides scale economies and a commanding share of the market as well as a stock of proprietary knowledge. These advantages also accrue to firms based in large nations where the domestic market is sufficiently large to enable them to achieve the full economies available. The size of the domestic market can be added to by foreign demand. An assured foreign demand can enable firms in small countries to achieve economies of scale and to be internationally competitive. The assurance of foreign demand is most easily obtained by the global production networks of multi-national enterprise that can allocate optimum size plants in accordance with the cost structures betokened by relative factor prices.[10]

Production functions are subject to the 'rules' of period analysis and change only in shifts. The change can comprise either an increase in the global stock of basic knowledge or a change in the modifier as the socio-economic characteristics of a nation evolve toward perfect economic rationality. Note that there are two kinds of increases in basic knowledge that are possible: an increase in man's technological knowhow, and a seepage into basic knowledge of (erstwhile) proprietary knowledge.

The complete production function for any good (i) in country j may be written as:

$$Q_i = s_i m_{ij} f_i (K, L, H, R, P) \qquad (3\text{-}3)$$

where s is the scalar determined by market size, m is the modifier that depends upon national characteristics, f is the input-mix function and the five variables in parentheses are the individual categories of factors of production.

---

[10] Willett has pointed out that multi-national enterprises added to the efficiency of global resource allocation in this way, see 'International Trade Theory is Still Relevant', p. 290.

TABLE 3-1

Summary of the Characteristics of the Three Trade Categories

Type of good	Basic cause of comparative advantage	Potential trade categories
1. Non-competitive	Inadequate availability in importing country of requisit specific factor	(i) Import (ii) Import and import augmenting good
2. Competitive, homogeneous	Endowments of general factors afford relative cost advantage	(i) Import (ii) Import and import competing good (iii) Export and domestic good
3. Differentiated	None necessary: but when trade consists wholly of exports or imports, comparative advantage will stem from general factor endowments	(i) Import, import-competing and export good (ii) Import and import-competing good (iii) Import (iv) Export and domestic good

THE INTEGRATION INTO THE MODEL OF THREE DIFFERENT TYPES OF GOOD

The three different types of goods to be included in the core theory are 'non-competitive' goods (type 1), 'ordinary' or homogenous competitive goods (type 2) and 'differentiated' goods (type 3). Each category has subclassifications. The basic features of the three generic categories are given in table 3-1.

Non-competitive goods (type 1) are goods whose elasticity of domestic supply at the going or any higher price and before complete specialization is zero. Non-competitive goods must necessarily require in their production some specific input that is either completely unavailable domestically or that is in limited supply domestically to the point that full utilization of the input will not satisfy domestic demand for the end product. Non-competitive goods cannot be exported.[11] They comprise three distinct subcategories.

---

[11] But see the comments on the grapes-in-Scotland concept below.

The first subcategory (good 1A) consists of products that cannot be physically produced domestically. All consumption must derive from imports. The specific factor prerequisite to the production of this type of good — presumably R but possibly P — is not domestically available. The specific input could be, in addition to R or P, a specific type of physical or human capital that will become available in a later period. Domestic supply is zero at any price and import reductions can only be accomplished by measures affecting domestic demand.

The second type of non-competitive good (1B) is one with positive domestic production but an elasticity of supply of zero at the going price. Import reductions can only be achieved by measures affecting domestic demand for the good. This type of good also requires a specific factor in its production but that input is not available in sufficient quantities for domestic self-sufficiency to be achieved at the going landed price of imports. Once some production of a good is possible because of the limited availability of the specific input, a sufficiently high tariff would make that good either a domestic good or a competitive good. This 'grapes-in-Scotland' concept may be eliminated by defining non-competitive goods as those for which total demand exceeds supply at the lowest positive price at which domestic supply is perfectly inelastic.[12] This type of commodity is most obviously represented by agricultural output in densely populated, intensively farmed, food-importing nations like Belgium, Japan, West Germany and the United Kingdom and by certain minerals such as nickel and oil in the United States. The concept of good 1B can be made more precise by figure 3-1. There, DD' and $S_d S_d$, are respectively the domestic demand and supply curves of a commodity requiring a specific input. $S_d EY$ is the total supply curve when no tariff is levied and $S_d HT$ is the total supply curve when an *ad valorem* tariff of $P_1 P_2 / OP_2$ is levied on imports. Domestic supply becomes completely inelastic at point H. At the free trade price, P_2, OA is produced domestically, AB are competitive imports and BG are non-competitive imports. At price P_1, all imports are non-competitive.[13]

---

[12] Note too that type 1B goods can conceivably be exported if intranational location factors are severe or if they are subject to seasonal factors.

[13] In practice, the possibility of competitive imports of type 1B goods can be ignored.

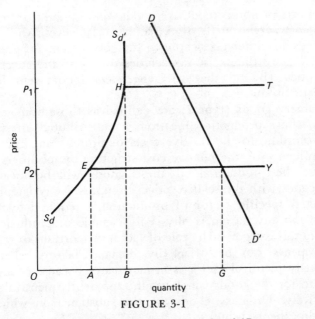

FIGURE 3-1

Non-competitive Imports of Good 1B

Type 1C goods require a certain technological expertise as a specific factor in their production and the lack of this necessary technology will debar domestic production of the good. Goods of this type will not necessarily continue to be non-competitive over time as P is imported or as the structure of society changes so that m changes to increase the ability to make use of basic knowledge. The composition of type 1C goods will vary over time as new, different goods are produced abroad and as older goods are increasingly capable of being produced within the focus nation.[14]

International trade in non-competitive goods has two quite distinct features that can affect the conclusions drawn from the orthodox model. First, there is a significant likelihood that international trade will involve the payment of a pure economic rent by residents of one nation to residents of another nation. This phenomenon can have important effects upon the magnitude and distribution of gains from trade. Second, the volume

[14] This process would correspond with the product cycle, see Raymond Vernon, 'International Investment and International Trade in the Product Cycle', *Quarterly Journal of Economics* 80, (May 1966), pp. 190–207.

of imports of non-competitive goods will respond identically to equal *ad valorem* tariffs or excise taxes. However, while all the proceeds of either tax accrue to the government for goods 1A and 1C, only the excise tax accrues totally to the government for goods 1B and the tariff engenders a quasi-rent for the domestic producer.

Ordinary goods (type 2) are defined as those homogeneous goods whose production locations are distributed internationally according to the relative costs of production. Except for any influence on the relative cost structure by modifiers or by scalars, the production of these goods will be located in accordance with the relative prices of inputs. No geographically restricted specific factor of production is required by type 2 goods and any nation is physically capable of producing any good in this category. The role of factor proportions or resource endowments can be offset by demand factors where the physically plentiful factor is in fact scarce because of a strong demand for the goods which use the apparently plentiful factor intensively. Ordinary goods are the substance on which the orthodox theory is built.

Differentiated goods (type 3) introduce into the general fabric of international trade theory, the dimension of imperfect or monopolistic competition. There exist many groups of goods among which the elasticity of substitution is very high without being infinite. Such goods are differentiated from each other by virtue of design, quality and selling-price differences but they are so closely competitive that they merit analysis as a group rather than as individual commodities.[15] The assumption of homogeneity makes price the unique determinant of trade. For differentiated goods competing in imperfect markets, price differences are no longer paramount. Because of the distinctions among goods, each good faces its own negatively sloped demand curve in each country.

Figure 3-2 shows the market conditions in A for a differentiated product manufactured in *B*. The demand curve is an

---

[15] Defining such groups is not easy. See E. H. Chamberlin, *The Theory of Monopolistic Competition* (6th ed.), (Cambridge: Harvard University Press, 1950), ch 1. Ohlin remarks upon the need for international trade theory to absorb this facet of analysis in 'Reflections', as does Harry G. Johnson in 'International Trade Theory and Monopolistic Competition Theory' in Robert E. Kuenne (ed.), *Monopolistic Competition Theory: Studies in Impact*, (New York: John Wiley and Sons, 1967), pp. 203–18.

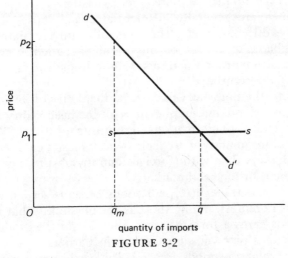

FIGURE 3-2

Trade in Differentiated Goods

equilibrium curve for a single period and its shape and position are determined by the prices and relative attractiveness of other goods in its group, by tastes and by the prices of all other goods. Since differentiated goods require a sales organization, there is some minimum quantity of goods, q_m, which must be sold to warrant the maintenance of a marketing organization in A. Thus, above price p_2 the demand schedule is not relevant and the supply schedule, ss, begins only at quantity, q_m. The supply schedule is shown as perfectly elastic at price p_1. The price, p_1, is the price of the product at A's frontier inclusive of import duties but exclusive of excise taxes and selling costs; it is determined by money costs of production in B and by the rate of exchange.[16]

Imports into A take place if $p_2 > p_1$. On the other hand, if $p_2 < p_1$, the good in question will not be traded from B to A. If B cannot export its differentiated good to A, it is probable that A enjoys a cost advantage in this type of good and will sell some of its production to B. It is also possible for two-way trade to take place in the good and for A to import and export goods within a group at the same time.[17]

[16] Selling costs are assumed to be internal to the country of sale. The money costs in B depend upon global resource allocation.
[17] See chapter 11 below.

Two types of differentiated goods can be distinguished — those which are generally differentiated and those which are nationally differentiated. The generally differentiated good (3A) can be either a final or an intermediate good. It competes in similar differentiated markets both at home and abroad. The nationally differentiated good (3B) reflects national tastes and tradition to the point at which the authenticity of its design, as denoted by its origin, supplies it with intrinsic utility in both domestic and foreign markets. Producers of type 3B goods compete more directly with their own domestic competitors in foreign markets than with (foreign) import-substitute producers for a segment of the total market.[18]

International trade in type 3 goods presents several analytic problems. Foremost among these is the possibility that trade in these goods earns a form of rental income for the producers of the good. This rent will derive from the barriers to entry in the market in which the goods are sold. The barriers are attributable to the advantage that accrues to an established firm in an imperfect market and from established marketing organizations and brand names. This rental income must be distinguished from income which accrues to proprietary knowledge. Proprietary knowledge will lower costs of production below those of competitors and generate a greater than average rate of return to equity capital. The latter is a return to research and development expenditures and can be earned by firms producing any of the three categories of goods. The former is a return to 'priority in the field' in a differentiated-goods industry.[19]

The determination of the rent derived from barriers to entry can be founded upon a variant of Chamberlin's large-group case. Constant returns to scale over the relevant range of output is assumed for all firms within the industry. When this assumption is made the comfortable tangency solution is lost and a determinate solution for an industry whose firms have perfectly elastic supply schedules, requires an additional or new variable. This is the quasi-rent ($q*$) of 'being in business'.

Consider an industry producing a differentiated good. Industry demand is determined by tastes, income and the set of

[18] Jacques Drèze emphasizes type 3B goods in 'Les exportations intra-C.C.E. en 1958 et la position belge', *Recherches économiques de Louvain* (1961), pp. 717–38.
[19] See Nicholas Kaldor, 'Market Imperfection and Excess Capacity', *Economica* n.s. (1935), pp. 33–50.

prices of all other goods. Assume that factor markets are perfect and that constant returns to scale prevail in all plants in the industry. Then the equilibrium of a single firm or plant can be represented by the pair of demand curves most commonly associated with the Chamberlinian model. In figure 3-3, the DD curve shows the demand curve facing the firm if it and all other firms in the industry change their prices proportionately: the dd curves show the demand facing the firm when only the focus alters its price. The costs, quality and design of products of all firms in the industry are assumed to be given in the absence of entry into or exit from the industry by other firms. If new firms enter, both demand curves shift to the left. Selling costs are ignored in figure 3-3 so that the schedules must assume constancy of selling effort and effectiveness by all firms and must represent receipts net of marketing costs.

Let a potential entrant into the industry require an expected rate of return on his investment in excess of that obtainable in an industry producing homogeneous goods. This excess will be required because of the greater uncertainty in a differentiated goods industry in which variability of tastes can combine with frequent design changes to make a firm more vulnerable to loss. Thus it is possible for firms in a differentiated-product industry to make a greater rate of return than firms in a homogeneous-product industry and still not to attract new entrants. The 'excess profit' per unit compatible with zero entry has some

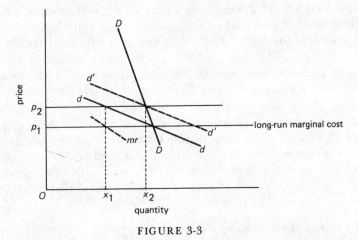

FIGURE 3-3

Equilibrium in a Differentiated Goods Market

limit, Q^*, which will vary with the industry and is determined exogenously to the model. It is possible for Q^* to vary within different segments of the same industry— high cost, low volume designs generating more uncertainty than the mass market.[20] Thus, provided $O < q^* < Q^*$ for all segments of the industry, no entry or exit will occur and an industry equilibrium is attainable.

Figure 3-3 demonstrates the attainment of that equilibrium. The individual firm attempts to maximize profits under the assumed independence of its pricing decisions and those of its competitors subject to the behavioural constraint that prices will not be raised when sales volume or market share is decreasing. Since $q^* > Q^*$ attracts new entrants into the appropriate segment of the market, the firm will not raise prices once $q^* > Q^*$. Consider the firm with the two solid demand curves shown in figure 3-3 and assume that $q^* < Q^*$. The firm will seek to maximize profits by producing x_1 at which marginal revenue is equal to marginal cost. The price charged will be p_2. (The assumption that $q^* < Q^*$ requires that $(p_2 - p_1) < Q^*$). If all firms react similarly, all will charge p_2 and expect to produce x_1. All firms will find that they can produce more. Although there may be some difficulty in attaining the equilibrium solution, the equilibrium for the focus firm (and all other identical firms) will be shown by the intersection of the solid demand curve, DD, and the dotted demand curve, dd. Price, p_2, and output, x_2, will be compatible with overall equilibrium. Now consider the equilibrium if, in this context, $(p_2 - p_1) > Q^*$. New entrants will be attracted to the industry and prices will stay at p_2 until self-interest and market pressures combine to force firms to reduce the price. The new entrants will select that part of the market closest in product design and quality to the firms making excess profits so that new entrants will affect the demand curve of those firms most directly.[21] The new product will be a closer substitute than any already on the market and $d'd'$ will revolve counter-clockwise as well as shift to the left with DD. The greater elasticity of the new flatter dd curve will bring about a

[20] In Kaldor's spatial version, *op. cit.*, pp. 390–91, Q^* will be greater at the ends of the ribbon.

[21] In Kaldor's spatial version, the new firms would locate between the two neighbours who were furthest apart.

reduction in the profit-maximizing price and this process will eventually assure that q^* is less than Q^* and entry will cease. The number of firms (manufacturing units) is not determinate and Q^* depends upon the estimation of uncertainty.

The existence of international trade does not affect this model. Foreign firms that are already established in the market will obey the same 'rules' as domestic firms. A foreign firm that is considering entry will not invest in the marketing organization unless the difference between its anticipated selling price and its landed cost is sufficient to ensure it a satisfactory return on its invested capital. It is possible in the period-analysis framework for the quasi-rent earned on imports to exceed Q^* for a single period. This would induce entry into the market by a domestic or a foreign firm in the ensuing period and the rent would decline in the following or a later period to less than q^*. International trade in differentiated goods must be assumed to allow for the quasi-rent to accrue to the exporter so that rent is paid internationally. However, sales costs are experienced in the country of sale so that selling costs themselves will not be included in the international trade model. Thus, exports of differentiated goods are made in line with administered prices. The level of those prices will be determined by marginal costs *and* by a premium bounded by entry considerations.

The gain derived from international trade in differentiated goods is less likely to be found in efficiency gains from the reallocation of factors of production on a global scale than from the wider choice offered to consumers in the importing country and from the discipline imposed upon the domestic industry by foreign competition. The foreign competition can generate increased x-efficiency, reduce opportunities for oligopolistic collusion and increase the innovative capacity of the domestic industry.

Most intermediate goods involve manufacturing processes and fall into the category of homogeneous goods in that the activity requires inputs that are generally available. The design of an intermediate good may be non-standard and may be produced to order for a manufacturer of differentiated goods but, if a special design is warranted, the volume of output will be sufficient for scale economies to be fully exploited. Thus, an engine part that is specially designed to fit into a differentiated product is not, in and of itself, differentiated in any operational way.

Two kinds of intermediate goods are differentiated: intermediate goods produced by one subsidiary of a multi-national enterprise for another subsidiary, and replacement parts for differentiated consumer durables. Replacement parts for consumer durables are differentiated in the sense that the marketing and distributional organization and access to inventories are limited to the original supplier of the durable good. Sales of this type of product are known as 'after-business'. These sales can and do command a premium in international trade so that an exporter will receive some quasi-rent similar in concept to the return on 'being in business'. International trade in intermediate products within a multi-national enterprise also permits an increase in profits (or lower costs) to be registered. This lowering of costs derives from economies internal to the multi-national enterprise — Coase-economies.[22] They affect the competitiveness of individual producers within a national rather than the relative competitiveness of producers located in different countries. There is, of course, no guarantee that the cost-saving and consequent quasi-rent will be allowed to accrue to the exporting subsidiary: the quasi-rent may be located almost at will by the multi-national enterprise.

Except for the possibility that biases in tastes will outweigh the effect of differences in resource endowments, the relationship between demand factors and the pattern of trade has never been closely reasoned. Demand is posited to be a function of tastes and income and tastes are exogenous to the model. Some concern has been registered over the effect of a change in tastes and growth models have realized the importance of increases in income on demand.[23] The few serious attempts to link trade patterns and demand have specified goods as the wage good or the non-wage good and, where income is free to vary, as necessities and luxuries. The introduction of specific factors of production that can earn rents from foreigners, and of the possibility of payments of quasi-rents makes the interrelation of a change in the pattern of output and a change in income distribution less easily identified. In much the same way, the

---

[22] See section 9 in chapter 2 above. See also my *The Economics of Business Investment Abroad* (London: Macmillan, 1972), pp. 77–81.

[23] See Caves, *Trade and Economic Structure*, ch. 7, for a review of the lack of depth of analysis of demand factors.

multiplicity of factors in the generalized theory will tend to weaken the analytic link that binds demand patterns to deduced changes in income distribution — unless the assumption is made that the 'poor' have only pure labour income and that payments for all other factors of production accrue to the 'rich'.

4 The Theory I:
From Autarky to Trade

The generalized theory is, in a large measure, derivative from the orthodox theory. However, the assumptions of the two theories are sufficiently different that the assumptions of the generalized theory must be set down clearly and explicitly before the theory can be developed.

THE ASSUMPTIONS

The primary assumption is that the theory is cast in terms of a short-run period-analysis model. The details of the version of period analysis to be used have been spelled out in chapter 3.

The analysis is limited to two countries.

Production functions are known: the input-mix elements are identical in both countries. Production functions can change between periods. Factors of production are assumed to have diminishing marginal rates of substitution, and substitutability is continuously differentiable.

With the exception of differentiated goods, all goods are sold in perfect markets. The money prices of the goods therefore reflect the marginal money costs of production. Factors of production are paid according to their marginal productivities determined in perfect factor markets with the exception of the return to proprietary knowledge. Differentiated goods prices may be influenced by the return to being in business and the earnings of proprietary knowledge explain any difference between money costs of production and selling price. Non-reproducible factors can earn an economic rent. This rent is attributed to a quality differential.

International transportation costs are assumed to be zero and location factors within nations are assumed to have no bearing on product availability or on factor prices.

Factors of production are assumed to be in fixed supply in any period but supply can migrate between countries at zero cost between periods. Factors are fully utilized.

Since the generalized theory must allow for natural resources, human capital and proprietary knowledge all to be industry-specific, the generalized theory is necessarily a multi-good theory. Goods with industry-specific inputs can be aggregated into categories of goods. These categories of non-competitive and differentiated goods can be aggregated and treated as (two) single trade categories despite the fact that individual component goods may have different industry-specific inputs.

Any core theory of international trade must aggregate dissimilar phenomena in order to achieve the needed degree of simplicity. The generalized theory aggregates goods into (a minimum of) three categories and the whole possible range of factors of production into (a minimum of) five categories. This aggregation process, particularly the aggregation of factors of production, rides roughshod over some conceptual problems.

The meaning of the concept of capital has been a bone of analytic contention in economics for many years and will, undoubtedly, continue to be so.[1] It is assumed that capital is identifiable as a factor of production in both its physical (K) and human (H) forms. It not assumed that one type of capital can be changed into another type of capital at short notice — within a period — but a redistribution of capital within the two categories can be brought about as depreciated capital is replaced and, over time, the ratio of the stock of human to physical capital can change.[2] Since factor supplies are assumed to be given in any particular period the reallocation of capital between periods derives from the dynamic aspects of period analysis. The mix of capital will be sensitive to any disparity to the returns to the two categories. The change in the supply of capital can be achieved by means of capital formation through time or follow from the international mobility of capital. Industry-specific capital — both human and physical — can acquire intra-marginal returns in the short run. There can be no guarantee that these quasi-rents will be eliminated in any particular time although, in the absence of some external disturbance, such quasi-rents will not increase over time and will generally decrease.

Natural resources (R) also present problems of aggregation.

[1] See Joan Robinson, 'The Measure of Capital', *The Economic Journal* 81, (September 1971), pp. 597–601.
[2] There is a clear debt to Peter B. Kenen's concepts here — see 'Nature, Capital and Trade', *op cit.*

Natural resources are essential to international trade in type 1*A* and type 1*B* non-competitive goods. Natural resources will either generate a rent for the owners of intramarginal units or, as in the case of climate, for the owners of the co-operating factors of production. At any time a nation can trade in and export more than one type of good requiring a specific factor of production and more than one non-reproducible resource will be involved in international trade within a single period. It is possible, and indeed likely, that both nations will import non-competitive goods simultaneously and therefore that rents will flow in both directions. The conceptual difficulties derive from the aggregation of the different natural resources within each country and from the process of netting out rents paid by the two nations within a single period. Payments of rent affect the internal distribution of income in both nations both before and after trade. International rent payments indicate a larger international gain from trade than would be derived from the same volume or value of trade in the absence of any rents. Net rents paid internationally will also affect the division of the global gain from trade. But the primary influence of net rental payments between nations will be on the overall competitiveness of a nation (through the rate of exchange) and therefore upon the pattern and direction of international trade.

Proprietary knowledge (*P*) is almost inevitably industry-specific. Like any industry-specific input, it will affect the relative costs and prices of different products differently in each country. In a multi-good framework, proprietary knowledge will affect the relative international competitiveness of different goods and industries. Since proprietary knowledge exists as a result of past outlays and endeavour, it is a costless asset in any period and the expansion of its use does not increase the total costs of the firm involved. Thus, the return to proprietary knowledge may be assumed to be constant per unit of output where constant costs and constant returns to scale apply. The return to proprietary knowledge has the characteristics of rent and its effect upon the pattern of trade and upon gains from trade is similar to that of natural resource endowments — except that proprietary knowledge can be moved internationally. It is assumed that the stock of proprietary knowledge used in a nation may be measured by aggregating its revenues. These revenues will accrue to the owners (who need not be the actual users) of the knowledge and will influence income distribution within and between the two countries.[3] Changes in the number of pieces of proprietary knowledge can take place between periods in response to new inventions and experience, international migration of knowhow and the lapse of patents.

Labour (L) is assumed to be homogeneous, except as improved by human capital, in both countries. Labour earns its marginal revenue product.

The theory assumes in this chapter that trade in current goods and services is balanced by the set of prices and the exchange rate reached at the end of each period. Where there are three separate categories of goods, the surplus on one category must equal the net deficit on the other two categories:

$$p_1 X_1 - p'_1 M_1 = p'_2 M_2 - p_2 X_2 + p'_3 M_3 - p_3 X_3 \qquad (4\text{-}1)$$

or

$$p_1 X_1 + p_2 X_2 + p_3 X_3 - (p'_1 M_1 + p'_2 M_2 + p'_3 M_3) = 0 \qquad (4\text{-}1\text{a})$$

where X and M stand for the quantities and p and p' for the prices of exports and imports respectively. The subscripts denote the category of goods. Category 1 goods must have positive R in the production function and may make use of P. Category 2 goods utilize only general factors of productions, $(K, L,$ and $H)$. Category 3, differentiated goods, will necessarily involve some proprietary knowledge in the course of production if only in the sense that design of a good constitutes a piece of proprietary knowledge. Category 3 goods will also earn the return for being in business for differentiated-goods firms.[4] For practical and conceptual purposes, the return to being in business is similar to the return to proprietary knowledge. Both are a species of rent constant per unit of output, both are given exogeneously and neither can be negative.

A multi-good or three-category model requires that there be a numeraire specified in each country that will allow the money prices of different goods to be compared. A rate of exchange between the two numeraires must also be specified. Money prices in national currencies are the obvious, but not the

---

[3] Prior to the introduction of unbalanced trade in goods and services, it is assumed that proprietary knowledge is owned by its users.
[4] See pp. 50–3 above.

inevitable choice for numeraire. The use of money prices obeys Ohlin's dictum that trade takes place because of differences in money prices and it moves the rate of exchange between the two currencies to centre stage. The rate of exchange will vary from period to period to establish balanced trade in goods and services. it is assumed that, while the relative prices of goods will change within both countries, absolute price levels do not change and the burden of adjusting the pattern of trade falls uniquely to the rate of exchange which is freely flexible.[5]

These are the assumptions, restrictions and conceptual underpinnings that limit the realism of the generalized theory. They also serve to make it useful as coherent body of thought. The next step is to evolve the generalized theory in the context of a movement from autarky to a situation of full trade.

THE THEORY

Consider a world of two autarkic nations. In both countries there will exist, at the end of any specified period, two sets of prices for goods and factors respectively. Select any rate of exchange between the two currencies and convert the autarkic prices of the second country into the first or focus country's currency. Compare the prices of the individual goods in the two countries. Non-competitive — types 1A and 1C — goods will not permit a direct comparison since, by definition, they cannot be produced in the importing country. Rank goods which can be produced in both countries according to the proportionate difference in their prices in the two autarkic countries, ranking goods which are cheaper in the focus country first. The focus country's type 1A and 1C potential exports will rank at the top of the list followed by goods in which the focus nation has the competitive edge. Further down the list will be goods which cost about the same in both countries and, at the bottom will be those goods in which the focus country is at a sizeable competitive disadvantage—including, at the very bottom, goods which the focus country cannot produce. The relative prices will be determined by factor supplies, technology, proprietary knowledge, tastes and income distribution in autarky.

[5] Speculation in foreign exchange is not permitted within the model though the model with unbalanced trade (see chapter 6) can be adapted to examine the effects of such speculation.

Now let international trade open up fully between the two nations. This will constitute a large disturbance and the prescribed assumption that equilibrium would be realized within one period is unrealistic. Period analysis is temporarily dispensed with and this part of the exposition can therefore be conducted in the traditional framework of general equilibrium. International *im*mobility of factors of production is assumed here. Given a flexible rate of exchange, there will be some rate of exchange that will balance trade in goods and services. Call that rate r^*. If the list of goods ranked in order of proportionate price differences is recomputed at the rate of exchange r^*, there is no requirement that the rank order will change. In that case, the goods in which the nation has a comparative advantage will be those which it supplies and sells more cheaply than the second country at r^*.[6] The rate of exchange, r^*, is equivalent, in the traditional model, to the critical factor-intensity ratio which determines the critical borderline good.[7] Comparative advantage derives from the same real factors that are included in the multi-factor orthodox model — resources, tastes, technology and income distribution.

When autarky gives way to trade, a very large disturbance is inaugurated. It is unlikely that the rank ordering of goods that existed in the autarkic situation will remain unchanged in the new equilibrium solution. The introduction of erstwhile unobtainable goods (types $1A$ and $1C$) can cause a fundamental alteration in the technologies available in both countries. These innovations will be capable of bringing about quite significant changes in the rank-ordering of commodities (and services) by competitiveness in the free-trade equilibrium. Thus, goods, which seemed to be destined to be exported could, because of the magnitude of the disturbance, turn out to be imports and a factor of production which appeared to be relatively plentiful in autarky could because of perverse output-mix effects and income effects, turn out to be relatively scarce in the free-trade equilibrium.

A movement from autarky to full trade will permit into both

[6] The concepts of ranking goods by competitiveness and of distinguishing between exports and imports by a dividing line belong to Frank Graham, *Readings in the Theory of International Trade*, p. 311.

[7] Cf. Samuelson, 'Theoretical Notes on Trade Problems', *Review of Economics and Statistics* (May 1964), p. 146.

countries the importation of previously unobtainable goods and proprietary knowledge. The knowledge may be either embodied in capital or intermediate goods or made available to the importing nation through licensing arrangements (the latter way is incompatible with the assumption of factor immobility). Provided that the non-competitive imports are primary or intermediate goods or (embodied) input-saving knowledge, the gain from trade will be of a different character and far greater than that portrayed by orthodox models. In terms of Meade's geometry which is the very essence of the two-good version of orthodoxy.[8] the opening of trade can bring about an increase in the size and a change in the shape of the production block (or surface) as well as involving an increase in world efficiency resulting from the reallocation of factors of production in both nations. The potential effect of international trade on the production complex may be more easily appreciated in a context of a reversion to autarky from a full-trade equilibrium. In addition to the painful disruptions inherent in the adjustment process, the new (autarkic) equilibrium would involve significantly lower levels of total output – particularly in small nations where the dependence upon non-competitive imports may be expected to be proportionately heavy.[9]

Orthodox theory emphasizes the change in the product mix that follows upon the opening of trade. Consequently the main area of enquiry is the change in the relative scarcity of factors of production and upon any change in their rates of reward. Comparative advantage derives from resources tastes, technology and income distribution. By virtue of increased production of the goods in which a comparative advantage exists, the relatively cheap factors experience increases in demand as a result of trade. This conclusion rests directly upon relatively passive assumptions about the impact of any change in total income or in relative factor returns upon the pattern of demand and upon the assumptions that production functions do not change in response to the opening up of trade.[10] In the strict

[8] James E. Meade, *A Geometry of International Trade* (London: George Allen and Unwin, 1952).

[9] Despite the fact that knowledge available prior to the reversion to autarky would still be available.

[10] The relatively small attention paid to the role of demand in international trade theory is noted by Caves in *Trade and Economic Structure*, ch. 6. Maximum

sense, production functions do not change as a result of the availability of erstwhile unobtainable goods or proprietary knowledge embodied in traded capital goods. However, for a nation with zero available inputs of certain natural resources and knowledge in a production function, what is feasible is only a 'partial' production function or input-mix element. The spaces or dimensions represented by the unavailable factors would be constrained at zero and the available domain of the production function is different in the two countries. When the non-competitive goods become available, the nation experiences what amounts to a change in its production function and it is quite possible that the relative factor intensity of the cooperating factors of production will change significantly. The anticipated change of relative prices of factors of production may not follow the general presumptions of the orthodox model. The pattern of demand may also change substantially as a result of so large a disturbance. Both the general increase in income resulting from the gain from trade as well as the redistribution of income can change the national tastes. When demand patterns change substantially, the ranking of goods by international competitiveness may differ from that which prevails in autarky so that it does not follow automatically that goods that appeared in autarky to be potential exports will, in fact, be exported in the full trade equilibrium.

There must be some predisposition to assume that the orthodox conclusions with respect to the consequences of trade for income distribution will hold in the aggregate. Changes in factor intensities as a result of 'changes' in production functions will apply to a relatively small proportion of goods produced and differences in tastes between different levels of income and among different factors must be quite strong if the change in the pattern of demand is to be sufficiently powerful to dominate variations in cost competitiveness in autarky. However, some marginal exports or imports in the autarkic ranking could be displaced by relatively small effects. Factors of production which are used relatively intensively in exported

---

heroism is achieved by Meade in his *Geometry* (p. 6) where he assumes that all consuming units have identical tastes and thereby annihilate the demand aspects of any income-distributional repercussions from changes in the volume or pattern of international trade.

goods will be designated as relatively plentiful factors and will experience higher rates of return under trade than in autarky. This will include returns paid to natural resources which are not available in the trading partner nation. It follows, automatically, from the existence of certain natural resources in only one nation of the two, that full factor price equalization cannot come about although the tendency toward relative and absolute equality of returns to generic factors of production will hold. Moreover, the conditions necessary for factor price equalization for those factors available in both countries cannot be generated.

The rank ordering of goods by competitiveness may change from autarky to full trade. The main factors affecting any such reranking of goods will be the possibility of 'different' production functions for some goods, different income elasticities of demand for different goods — given the change in income and income distribution that follow from trade — and differences in supply elasticities of individual goods. Since the assumption of ubiquitous constant returns to scale has been discarded and since some natural resources that are industry-specific can vary by quality of mineral deposit and have quite small elasticities of supply, some goods may have such small elasticities of supply that only a small increase in demand is enough to induce a sizeable change in relative competitiveness.

The roles of scalars and modifiers in the determination of the ranking can also be important. In addition to the possible influence of varying returns to scale upon the supply elasticities of individual goods, scale effects are quite likely to determine the ranking of a good in autarky. In those industries in which increasing returns to scale apply, the larger the industry the lower will be the average and marginal costs of production. Thus, when full trade is instituted, the autarkic scale of opertion in the two countries will be likely to determine which country has the lower money costs. Moreover, the cost advantage will be enhanced when foreign demand is added to domestic demand and further scale economies achieved. This scale effect is also likely to outweigh any disadvantage from differences in relative input prices that may be enjoyed by the small scale producer. A scale advantage accrues to larger and richer nations both when trade is instituted at some specified time and when a nation has a temporal priority in the development and production of the good in question. Scale advantages of this kind are the basis for the argument for infant-industry protection and for the concept of the product cycle.[11] Scale effects can transform a good from one which might be expected to be produced in both countries to one countries to one for which demand is fully satisfied by imports in the smaller nation. Modifiers will tend to make goods non-competitive (type 1C). It is quite possible that, in the absence of socio-economic differences between nations, a good would be capable of production in both countries. Because of those differences, the production function for the good is so modified that production becomes virtually impossible. The good then becomes one of the bottom-ranked goods for the potential importer.

In addition to the two sources of gains from trade referred to above, there is a third source — when rental income accrues to a nation because it sells natural resources to foreigners. Any excess of return paid to a factor over and above its transfer price represents a rent or stream of income in excess of any 'cost' of production and is therefore a return achieved without effort.[12] The source of rent is scarcity and can derive from either location or qualitative differences. For the purpose of explaining its role in gains from trade, it will be presumed that natural resource deposits are of different qualities. Once natural resources enter into international trade, either directly or indirectly in the form of goods that contain the natural resources, the natural resources may earn a rent for their owners. To the extent that this rent is paid by foreigners it increases national income as if by a windfall process. The rent in this example would be computed as the rent earned on the units sold to foreigners: this will be less than the total rent earned and less than the increase in rent earned. If both countries import non-competitive goods, and pay rent to their trading partners, gains from trade will be *pro tanto* increased. Income distribution will also be affected by the size of any rent component in national income. Similar gains from trade accrue as a result of the licensing of proprietary knowledge which can

---

[11] See Raymond Vernon, 'International Investment and International Trade in the Product Cycle', *Quarterly Journal of Economics* 80, (May 1966), pp. 190–207.

[12] For the authoritative review of rent see Joan Robinson, *The Economics of Imperfect Competition*, (London: Macmillan and Company, 1933), ch. 8.

be used abroad without incurring any further cost. Quasi-rents paid to exporters of differentiated goods as a return to being in business will expand gains from trade. However, as noted above, the gain from trade that results from international trade in differentiated goods is probably qualitatively different from the gains that derive from trade in type 1 and type 2 goods.[13]

The concept of rank-ordering goods by comparative advantage recalls Graham's two-country four-commodity model except that Graham's rigid demand conditions and the assumption of constant costs are not imposed upon the generalized theory outlined here.

> If we should arrange in a column the names of the commodities consumed by any given country, placing at the top and at the bottom, respectively, the two commodities in which the country showed the widest difference in productive power when compared with the foreign trading world in general, then, taking the commodity last on the list as a base, and measuring in the same way, should set down in the order of diminishing difference in productive power all the commodities lying between the two originally selected, we should have a list in which that country would have a comparative advantage in the production of any commodity on the list over all the commodities which succeeded it, and a comparative disadvantage, therefore, with regard to all the commodities which preceded it. But the line dividing national comparative advantage and disadvantage might settle anywhere between the two extreme commodities, and would shift from time to time as the terms of exchange of international products moved in one direction or the other.[14]

Graham's concepts were valuably transformed into familiar Marshallian offer curves. Because of the two assumptions of demand patterns and constant costs, the derived offer curves had steps and risers rather than the smooth shape compatible with a philosophy of *natura non facit saltum*. The generalized

[13] See above, p. 53.
[14] Frank D. Graham, 'The Theory of International Values Reexamined', particularly p. 311. The transformation of the model is performed by G. A. Elliott, 'The Theory of International Values', *Journal of Political Economy*, (February 1950), pp. 16–29.

theory can be expressed in offer curves in much the same ways as Graham's model. The rate of exchange will be determined by the intersection of the two offer curves. The difference lies in the greater complexity inherent in the generation of the offer curves. The possibility that marginal costs rise slowly with output allows for many goods to be produced simultaneously in both countries in the full trade equilibrium. Graham's model only allows for the single good to be produced in both countries and uses this equality of costs and the conjecture of the two offer curves that it typified, to explain the stability of the rate of exchange in the real world. If, instead, many goods are produced in both countries under conditions of slowly rising supply schedules, the international price mechanism will be quite sensitive to changes in the rate of exchange and there is no need for a 'one-good conjuncture' in its pure form. However, Graham is correct in stating that the redistribution of production in quite closely competitive goods can provide a sizeable amount of adjustment with only a small change in the terms of trade.[15]

When the multi-good, generalized theory is used to explain the transformation from autarky to a full trade equilibrium, the ultimate solution cannot be spelled out succinctly and tidily without highly restrictive assumptions being introduced. The movement is a large one and the generalized theory envisages the possibility of too many potentially perverse relationships. Any perversities that may exist will probably not be sufficiently strong to overpower a tendency toward equalization of the prices of generic factors. The explicit introduction into the analysis of non-competitive goods adds two different sources of gains from trade to the source of gain in the orthodox model. The receipt of rents and quasi-rents from foreigners and the potential increase in technology and in the feasible domains of individual production functions will both add to the global gains from trade. The generalized theory, because of its reference to industry-specific factors of production, must be a multi-good theory and this is, in turn, the source of its generality. Some of the axioms derived from the orthodox model will have to be qualified.

---

[15] The concept of a multi-commodity offer curve is developed in chapter 5.

A SIMPLIFIED, FORMAL MODEL

To concoct a simple version of the generalized theory requires the sacrifice of some of its important features. To be manageable in a formal sense, the model must be stripped to the bone and must retain only the most broadly applicable characteristics of the generalized theory. The short-run, period adjustment frame of reference is discarded in favour of the timeless, general equilibrium concept used to consider the change from autarky to full trade. Period analysis is reserved for analysis of the behaviour of the system when small changes disturb an ongoing full trade equilibrium.[16] To reduce the number of goods to a minimum, all industry-specific forces are excluded from the simple model. Thus, scalars and modifiers are ignored, human capital is merged into a generic factor of production with physical capital, and proprietary knowledge is discarded from the frame of reference.

The model involves five goods (three categories of goods) and three factors of production. The five goods consist of one type 1 good imported by country A (a type $1A$ good), two competitive goods (2.1 and 2.2) that can be produced in each country and two type 3 goods which compete closely with each other; good 3.1 is made in country A and good 3.2 in B. Production functions for the two type 3 goods are different because the goods are different. Type 2 and type 3 goods are produced with two homogeneous, general factors of production (capital and labour). These factors are in fixed supply in each country and are traded in perfect markets so that each receives its marginal value product in the production of type 2 goods. Type 1 and type 2 goods are both sold at prices equal to marginal cost and command the same price in both countries. Differentiated goods are sold at marginal cost plus some constant (q_i) determined exogenously for each good in each country. Country A's non-competitive import utilizes a specific factor of production available only in country B, $_BS$. This factor is a natural resource which varies in quality in a known manner and which has a transfer price of zero. The cost of the non-competitive good is determined by the marginal cost of production which increases with the quantity produced because of the positively sloped supply schedule of $_BS$. Intramarginal

---

[16] See chapter 5 below.

units of S earn a rent and the total rent is determined by the total quantity of S produced per period of time — the relationship between the supply of S and its marginal cost being determined exogeneously.[17] The form of the production function for the non-competitive good requires that the marginal physical product of capital and labour in the production of the type 1 good is less than their average product. The difference between the value of total output or sales of the type 1 good and the total payments to labour and capital constitute the total rent earned by $_B S$.

In accordance with the assumptions set out in the first part of this chapter, domestic currencies are used as the numeraires and balanced trade is maintained by means of a freely fluctuating rate of exchange between the two currencies. The equilibrium rate of exchange is determined by real variables and by market structures and any change in the underlying demand and supply configurations will bring about a change in the rate of exchange. If the disturbance takes place in the production or sale of a type 2 good such that country A will experience a trade deficit prior to adjustment, A's currency must be assumed to depreciate. The price of the non-competitive good will increase in A's currency and the balance of trade in type 3 goods will change in A's favour. Similarly, if the disturbance occurs in the output or sale conditions of type 3 goods, the balance of trade on type 2 goods will move in A's favour. In this way the rent earned by B from exports of the non-competitive good and the net proprietary rent earned on the trade of type 3 goods both respond to changes in the rate of exchange

Equations for the Formal Model

The formal model comprises forty-seven equations. Of these, only forty-four are independent.

Letting $_A K$ and $_A L$ represent total available capital and labour in A respectively, the quantity of capital (labour) devoted to the production of a particular good (type 2, number 1) in B can be written as $_b k_{21}$.

---

[17] In Joan Robinson's terms, this is a γ cost curve: see *The Economics of Imperfect Competition*, p. 134.

$$_AK = {_ak_{21}} + {_ak_{22}} + {_ak_{31}} \tag{4-2}$$

$$_BK = {_bk_1} + {_bk_{21}} + {_bk_{22}} + {_bk_{32}} \tag{4-3}$$

$$_AL = {_al_{21}} + {_al_{22}} + {_al_{31}} \tag{4-4}$$

$$_BL = {_bl_1} + {_bl_{21}} + {_bl_{22}} + {_bl_{32}} \tag{4-5}$$

$$_BS = {_bs_1} \tag{4-6}$$

The five production functions are given and outputs are denoted by z so that $_bz_1$ denotes the output of the type 1 good in B.

$$_az_{21} = \psi_{21}({_ak_{21}}, {_al_{21}}) \tag{4-7}$$

$$_az_{22} = \psi_{22}({_ak_{22}}, {_al_{22}}) \tag{4-8}$$

$$_az_{31} = \psi_{31}({_ak_{31}}, {_al_{31}}) \tag{4-9}$$

$$_bz_1 = \psi_1({_bs_1}, {_bk_1}, {_bl_1}) \tag{4-10}$$

$$_bz_{21} = \psi_{21}({_bk_{21}}, {_bl_{21}}) \tag{4-11}$$

$$_bz_{22} = \psi_{22}({_bk_{22}}, {_bl_{22}}) \tag{4-12}$$

$$_bz_{32} = \psi_{32}({_bk_{22}}, {_bl_{32}}) \tag{4-13}$$

Equilibrium in production requires that the payment to each general factor equal its marginal value productivity in each industry. The payment to factor K is u, to factor L is w and factor S earns rent equal to V in total. Proprietary rents, $_aq_{31}$ and $_bq_{32}$, are given exogenously. Primed monetary variables denote values expressed in B's currency.

$$_au = p_{21}(\delta\psi_{21}/\delta k_{21}) = p_{22}(\delta\psi_{22}/\delta k_{22})$$
$$\tag{4-14}(4-15)$$

$$_aw = p_{21}(\delta\psi_{21}/\delta l_{21}) = p_{22}(\delta\psi_{22}/\delta l_{22})$$
$$\tag{4-16}(4-17)$$

$$_bu' = p'_1(\delta\psi_1/\delta k_1) = p'_{21}(\delta\psi_{21}/\delta k_{21}) = p'_{22}(\delta\psi_{22}/\delta k_{22})$$
$$\tag{4-18}(4-19)(4-20)$$

$$_bw' = p'_1(\delta\psi_1/\delta l_1) = p'_{21}(\delta\psi_{21}/\delta l_{21}) = p'_{22}(\delta\psi_{22}/\delta l_{22})$$
$$\tag{4-21}(4-22)(4-23)$$

$$p_{31} = {_aq_{31}} + {_au}(\delta k_{31}/\delta\psi_{31}) + {_aw}(\delta l_{31}/\delta\psi_{31}) \tag{4-24}$$

$$\frac{\delta\psi_{31}/\delta k_{31}}{\delta\psi_{31}/\delta l_{31}} = \frac{\delta\psi_{21}/\delta k_{21}}{\delta\psi_{21}/\delta l_{21}} \tag{4-25}$$

$$p'_{32} = {}_b q'_{32} + {}_b u'(\delta k_{32}/\delta\psi_{32}) + {}_b w'(\delta l_{32}/\delta\psi_{32}) \tag{4-26}$$

$$\frac{\delta\psi_{32}/\delta k_{32}}{\delta\psi_{32}/\delta l_{32}} = \frac{\delta\psi_{22}/\delta k_{22}}{\delta\psi_{22}/\delta l_{22}} \tag{4-27}$$

$$_a q_{31} = {}_a q_{310} \tag{4-28}$$

$$_b q_{32} = {}_b q_{320} \tag{4-29}$$

$$_b V' = {}_A X_1 \cdot p'_1 + {}_B X_1 \cdot p'_1 - {}_b u' \cdot {}_b k_1 - {}_b w' \cdot {}_b l_1 \tag{4-30}$$

Equation (4-30) states that total rent accruing to the specific factor is equal to the total revenue from the sale of the type 1 good less the payments to general factors of production in that industry. Quantities consumed are represented by X. The rate of exchange must be explicit[18] and is defined as equating the prices of goods in both countries in a common numeraire.

$$p_1 = p'_1 \cdot r \qquad (\text{or } p_{21} = p'_{21} \cdot r) \tag{4-31}$$

Money income is denoted by Y and all income generated is spent.

$$_A Y = {}_a w_A L + {}_a u_A K + {}_a q_{31} \cdot {}_a z_{31} = r p'_1 \cdot {}_A X_1 + p_{21} \cdot {}_A X_{21}$$
$$+ p_{22} \cdot {}_A X_{22} + p_{31} \cdot {}_A X_{31} + r p'_{32} \cdot {}_A X_{32} \tag{4-32}$$

$$_B Y = {}_b w'_B L + {}_b u'_B K + {}_B V' + {}_b q'_{32} \cdot {}_b z_{32} = p'_1 \cdot {}_B X_1$$
$$+ p'_{21} \cdot {}_B X_{21} + p'_{22} \cdot {}_B X_{22} + p_{31}/r \cdot {}_B X_{31} + p'_{32} \cdot {}_B X_{32} \tag{4-33}$$

Demand functions for each good can be written as the ratio of money expenditure upon the good to total money income. Demand is a function of relative prices and there are five demand equations for each country. In each set of five, only four equations are independent. Relative prices are denoted by P. The price, $_A P_{21}$, is a conglomerate notation summarizing the

---

[18] See Caves, *Trade and Economic Structure*, p. 39.

equilibrium values of the other four prices: rp'_1, p_{22}, p_{31} and rp'_{32}.

$$(rp'_1 \cdot {}_A X_1)/_A Y = {}_a\phi_1(rp'_1/_A P_1) \tag{4-34}$$

$$(p_{21} \cdot {}_A X_{21})/_A Y = {}_a\phi_{21}(p_{21}/_A P_{21}) \tag{4-35}$$

$$(p_{22} \cdot {}_A X_{22})/_A Y = {}_a\phi_{22}(p_{22}/_A P_{22}) \tag{4-36}$$

$$(p_{31} \cdot {}_A X_{31})/_A Y = {}_a\phi_{31}(p_{31}/_A P_{31}) \tag{4-37}$$

$$(rp'_{32} \cdot {}_A X_{32})/_A Y = {}_a\phi_{32}(rp'_{32}/_A P_{32}) \tag{4-38}$$

$$(rp'_1 \cdot {}_B X_1)/_B Y' = {}_b\phi_1(rp'_1/_B P'_1) \tag{4-39}$$

$$(rp'_{21} \cdot {}_B X_{21})/_B Y' = {}_b\phi_{21}(rp'_{21}/_B P'_{21}) \tag{4-40}$$

$$(rp'_{22} \cdot {}_B X_{22})/_B Y' = {}_b\phi_{22}(rp'_{22}/_B P'_{22}) \tag{4-41}$$

$$(p_{31}/r \cdot {}_B X_{31})/_B Y' = {}_b\phi_{31}(p_{31}/r/_B P'_{31}) \tag{4-42}$$

$$(rp'_{32} \cdot {}_B X_{32})/_B Y' = {}_b\phi_{32}(rp'_{32}/_B P'_{32}) \tag{4-43}$$

Finally, five more equations are necessary to describe the process of the equating of world demands for and supplies of each commodity.

$$_b z_1 = {}_A X_1 + {}_B X_1 \tag{4-44}$$

$$_a z_{21} + {}_b z_{21} = {}_A X_{21} + {}_B X_{21} \tag{4-45}$$

$$_a z_{22} + {}_b z_{22} = {}_A X_{22} + {}_B X_{22} \tag{4-46}$$

$$_a z_{31} = {}_A X_{31} + {}_B X_{31} \tag{4-47}$$

$$_b z_{32} = {}_A X_{32} + {}_B X_{32} \tag{4-48}$$

Of these forty-seven equations, only forty-four are independent. In addition to the 'loss' of two equations in the sequence (4-34) to (4-43), only six equations from the set (4-32), (4-33), and (4-44) to (4-48) are independent. There are also forty-four unknowns; fourteen comprise the allocation of the two general factors to seven production processes ($7k$'s and $7 l$'s); seven levels of output ($7 z$'s); ten rates of consumption of five goods ($10 X$'s); five prices ($5 p$'s); four rates of return to factors ($2 u$'s and $2 w$'s); three rents ($2 q$'s and V') and a rate of exchange (r). Such an equality between independent equations and variables is compatible with a solution yielding an economic equilibrium but guarantees neither the solution nor its uniqueness.[19]

[19] The existence of a unique solution is assumed.

In the model, the rate of exchange, r, serves as an index for the net barter terms of trade. The equilibrium rate that produces balanced trade in goods and services is, as may be expected for a balancing item, determined by a large number of variables.

$$r^* = r(_B V', _A Y, _B Y', _A X_1, p'_1, p_{21}, p_{31}, p'_{32},$$
$$q_{31}, q'_{32}, _A X_{32}, _B X_{31}) \quad (4\text{-}49)$$

CONCLUSION

The application of the generalized theory to the analysis of the transition from autarky to full trade has shown that the gains from trade are likely to have been seriously underestimated by the orthodox theory. The introduction into the analysis of natural resources and proprietary knowledge create the possibility of the existence of non-competitive goods and unavailable technology. From the existence of such goods derives not only the possibility of new methods of production but, in addition, the rental income that will accrue to one or both nations.

The introduction of many (five) factors of production clearly limits the degree of confidence with which the effects of international trade on the relative returns to general factors of production can be deduced. The existence of commodity-specific inputs allows for goods with seemingly perverse factor intensities as far as the general factors are concerned, to be traded internationally. In the orthodox model, all goods that are, say, more labour-intensive than some critical or borderline goods, will be exported and those less so, imported. Perverse factor-intensity can apply only to general factors of production such as labour and capital. In terms of the notation of the formal model given above, perverse factor-intensity will be defined to exist when an export from a capital-scarce country (B) uses a higher ratio of capital-to-labour than does the marginal type 2 export. Equally, perverse factor-intensity can apply to imports of type 1, 2 and type 3 goods when B's import-competing industries use a higher ratio of labour-to-capital than the marginal type 2 export. It would seem that the feasible degree of factor perversity will be less for differentiated goods than for type 1 goods. In the simplest version in which the only proprietary knowledge used in the differentiated good is a design difference, differentiated goods have only the slope of the foreign demand curve to counteract cost or price differences. If, however, the production function is more complex and the general factors combine with some production technology, then differentiated goods may be as capable of factor perversity as are type 1 goods.

The effect of the opening of international trade on income distribution can, where type 1 goods are traded and/or perverse factor-intensities hold, can qualify the traditional analysis of the effect of trade on income distribution. The most important difference will be the increased return earned by the specific input used in the type 1 export. Depending upon the rate of qualitative deterioration of the input as the volume of output of the type 1 good increases, rent will accrue to the intramarginal units as total demand for the end product increases with the inauguration of foreign demand. The greater this demand and the greater the rate of qualitative deterioration of the marginal specific inputs, the greater will be the increase in the total earnings of that factor of production. It is not impossible that the specific factor will enjoy the largest absolute *and* proportionate increase in income.[20] If type 1 or type 3 exports involve perverse factor-intensities, and if the focus nation has a trade surplus on type 3 goods, then the gain to the plentiful factor of production from the institution of international trade will be smaller than in the absence of that factor perversity. It is possible that factor perversity and exports of the type 1 and type 3 goods could combine to make the seemingly scarce general factor of production enjoy an increase in its return relative to that seemingly plentiful factor. Such an untoward outcome would require high degrees of factor perversity coupled with a large proportion of total trade being carried out in type 1 and type 3 goods.

---

[20] This result is not surprising since the specific factor is, relatively, the scarcest.

5 The Theory II:
The Adjustment Process

A comparison between the output and consumption patterns of two nations in autarky and under conditions of full trade does provide a basis for proving the existence of gains from trade and for estimating the distribution of those gains between nations. The comparison also allows for the income-distributional effects of the inauguration of international trade to be analysed. However, the comparison is based upon a gross disturbance and there can be no certainty, in a multi-commodity model, that the rank-ordering of goods (by comparative advantage) under autarkic conditions does not change to an important degree during the process of transition from autarky to full trade. The implications of changes in the rank ordering of goods are that any conclusions drawn from the model about the mix or structure of international trade must be hedged in with *caveats*. For example, a good that appeared in autarky to be an exportable might, under conditions of full trade, turn out to have such inelastic domestic supply and such a high domestic income elasticity of demand that the good is, in fact, imported. These reservations about the validity of the comparison also apply when the analysis is applied to income-distributional questions and the strong factor-intensity assumption is not imposed upon the analysis — as would be foolhardy in a multi-factor world in which not all factors are used in all goods.

A frame of reference that is more appropriate to modern concerns with international trade is the examination of the consequences of and the process of adjustment to specified, relatively small disturbances that follow from minor changes in the underlying data — or even from absolutely quite large changes. In a period analysis framework, these disturbances can be autonomous or they can be 'derived' — that is they follow from the characteristics of the short-run equilibrium achieved at the end of the previous period and from a discrepancy between the short-run and potentially long-run equilibria. Ignoring for the time being the possibility of man-made disturbances such as changes in tariff structures, the disturbances can affect either the supply or the demand patterns in either or both countries. Furthermore the disturbances can be classified as involving either *general* changes that affect all goods produced or demanded or *industry-specific* changes in which only one good (or a small group of related goods) is directly affected by the change in the underlying data. For example, an increase in the supply of labour in one country would constitute a general disturbance; it would affect the wage and, through that, the money costs of all goods produced in that country. The increase in the supply of labour might or might not affect the relative competitiveness of different goods in international trade but it will affect the net barter terms of trade at which balanced trade will be achieved, r^*, or the absolute price levels prevailing in the two countries. A change in r^* indicates a change in the net barter terms of trade needed for balanced trade. On the demand side, an increase in income in a country would be a general disturbance. An industry-specific change will take place when the supply of some industry-specific natural resource is altered and this will change the relative-competitiveness of different goods in international trade and, therefore, the mix of goods traded, A change in tastes, involving an increase in the demand for one good and a concomitant reduction in the demand for another single good or from all other goods, constitutes an industry-specific disturbance on the demand side of the equation. Once again the ranking of goods by international competitiveness will be likely to change. This distinction between general and industry-specific disturbances is of primary importance — particularly for the incorporation of direct international investment into the analytic framework. The distinction can best be approached by casting the analysis in terms of a multi-commodity offer curve. The essence of the reliance upon this familiar analytic device will be to indicate the fact that industry-specific changes will be likely to induce change in the shape as well as in the position of a nation's offer curve. In addition, the offer curve analysis will demonstrate the interdependence of the market for all goods to both general and specific changes in the underlying data — thus the prosperity of one or of all industries can be directly affected by changes in the international supply—demand configurations of another industry.

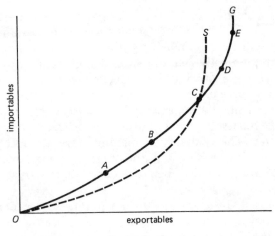

FIGURE 5-1

A Multi-commodity Offer Curve

A MULTI-COMMODITY OFFER CURVE

The offer curve can be used to show how the trading and production patterns will adjust to disturbances in both the focus (domestic) nation and in the trading partner. The offer curve shows the volume of trade a nation is willing to conduct at different commodity terms of trade. It is shown in figure 5-1 with its familiar shape. The solid curve, *OG*, represents the original offer curve and a shift of the offer curve will therefore indicate a general disturbance. The dotted curve, *OS*, represents a new offer curve after an industry-specific disturbance has occurred. The multi-commodity offer curve traces it heritage to Graham and to Elliott's adaptation of Graham's construct.[1] In the offer curve, diminishing marginal utility is ascribed to each imported good and each production unit is assumed to have a positively sloped (or non-negatively sloped) marginal cost schedule. Any change in technology and in the availability of certain type 1 imports made possible by international trade is assumed to have been achieved — full trade is assumed to have been established. In the segment of the offer curve, *OA*, the net barter terms of trade are so adverse to the focus country that it finds only a very small number of foreign

[1] See pp. 81—2 above.

goods cheaper than their domestically-produced substitutes. It will probably import only a small number of different goods and these will be dominated by non-competitive imports. The nation is theoretically able to export a large number of different commodities (the dividing line is very low in the ranking) but the demand for exports is small and therefore the volume of trade remains small as represented by point A. The exports may be spread, relatively evenly, over a wide range of individual commodities. The diminishing marginal rate of substitution of imports for exportables and the increasing marginal costs of exports combine to give the offer curve some curvature in the *OA* segment.

For point *B* to be an equilibrium point, foreign demand for focus-country exports must have increased due to a (general) disturbance in the trading-partner country. The terms of trade will have improved and the dividing line shifted upward. More foreign goods will now be able to compete successfully with domestic production and the values of imports has increased. The mix of these imports and of the concomitant exports will derive from money-price considerations. The mix will, therefore, depend upon the (total) elasticities of demand for *all* internationally traded goods in both countries — both price and income elasticities. The mix will also depend upon the output- and price-elasticities of supply of the traded goods in the two countries. Define the sensitivity of a good to the terms of trade as the change in the volume of imports or exports of that good per unit change in the terms of trade. Sensitivity will be a function of the way in which supply and demand for each good react to the change in the terms of trade *and* to the disturbance that has induced the change in the terms of trade. Sensitivity, then, is a function of foreign price and income elasticities and domestic price and income elasticities of demand and of the equivalent supply elasticities. The trading mix at point *B* will depend upon the relative sensitivities of the different goods traded.

The sensitivity of an imported good will be greater, the greater are the price and income elasticities of demand for that good in the importing country and the smaller the price and output-elasticities of supply in that same country. The greater the price- and output-elasticities of excess foreign supply, the greater will the sensitivity of that good be. The sensitivity of an

export will have the reverse relationships. The greater the price-
and income-elasticities of domestic demand and the smaller
price- and output-elasticities of domestic supply, the less will be
the elasticity of excess supply for foreign markets and the less
sensitive will that good tend to be. Graham, in his two-country
multi-commodity analysis, imposed such specific demand and
supply conditions upon the model that the problem of changing
mixes in tradeable goods was eliminated.[2]

The mix of exports and imports at point B will influence the
short-run profitability of the different industries engaged in
international trade. As r^* shifts upwards, the focus nation will
export a smaller number of an import a larger number of
individual goods. In both cases the volume of goods traded has
increased. Not every exported good will inevitably enjoy an
increase in the volume of international trade. Thus, the
profitability of different industries, in both the short run and
the long run, is affected by the mix of goods and therefore by
the sensitivities of goods to changes in the terms of trade. One
important determinant of the mix of exports at point B is the
new pattern of foreign demand that must exist for point B to be
an equilibrium trading point (in the short run) and another is
the correlation of that pattern with the export supply characteristics of the focus country's industries. By postulating that the
disturbance bringing about the necessary shift in the foreign
offer curve is 'general', net foreign demand for focus-country
exports will have increased evenly across the spectrum of
exports. This is not a precise statement and it brings out an
important analytic point. Because the quantity of any good
demanded from abroad at given terms of trade depends upon
the elasticities of both supply and demand in both countries,
the position of point B and therefore of the offer curve itself,
depends upon conditions in both nations.[3] There is then, for
multi-commodity offer curves, an interdependency that must
qualify the use of offer curves in analyses of international trade
and of any other approaches that rest upon similar constructs
and assumptions.

Multi-commodity offer curves cannot properly be drawn with

---

[2] See Graham, *loc. cit.*, and Elliott, *loc. cit.*
[3] If transport costs create non-traded goods, the interaction of demand and supply
factors with this set of goods is also important. A simple adaptation is presented in
chapter 6.

reference only to the demand and supply conditions that exist
in the focus country. Provided different goods have different
sensitivities to changes in the terms of trade and if industry-
specific factors exist offer curves must be drawn as a series of
intersections of foreign and domestic reciprocal demands at
varying terms of trade. The proposition that offer curves relate
only to the focus nation (a proposition exemplified by Meade's
derivation of the offer curve in his geometric treatment of
international trade) does not hold when more than two goods
are included in the analytic framework. A nation's offer curve is
uniquely determinable only when the complete set of foreign
demand and supply functions is known and, in turn, these
foreign demand characteristics can only be known once the
pattern of focus-country excess demand and supply functions
for individual goods has been defined for all terms of trade.
Even more restrictive is the problem alluded to above – the
cause of the shift in the foreign offer curve that instigates the
change in the equilibrium terms of trade must be exactly
defined. The multi-commodity offer curve must, therefore, be a
series of intersections between two offer curves. If conditions in
the focus country are considered to be unchaging, the shift of
the foreign offer curve can be caused by a variety of
disturbances (general and industry-specific) and each of these
may cause a different trading posture on the part of the focus
nation. A shift in the foreign offer curve can bring about a
corresponding shift in the focus-country curve. Thus, strictly, it
is not possible to conceive of a unique shape for a multi-
commodity offer curve for a nation. But the concept of an offer
curve is still useful. Almost inevitably a disturbance will induce
a larger shift in the offer curve of the country in which the
disturbance has taken place than in the offer curve of the
trading partner.[4] Thus, except for quite dramatic disturbances
originating in the foreign country, it will be possible to derive a
multi-commodity offer curve for a nation on the presumption
that induced effects are negligible. Further, the concept of a
general disturbance is still useful. A general disturbance in a
country will change the position of that country's offer curve

---

[4] The neoclassical analyses relying upon bales of productive factors are not subject
to this qualification but the Marshallian concept of bales loses much of its value when
industry-specific natural resources have to be included in the bales.

more that its shape and the reaction of the foreign nation's offer curve will also affect position more than shape.

If the analytic problem of possible induced shifts in *OG* in figure 5-1 is disregarded, the effect of movement along *OG* to points *C*, *D*, and *E* can be considered briefly. As the terms of trade continue to move in favour of the domestic nation, the number of individual goods imported continues to increase and the number exported to decline. But the proportionate mix of goods at each of these points continues to depend upon demand and supply conditions in both kinds of goods in both countries. Further, demand conditions can change as a result of income distribution as well as by changes induced either by autonomous changes or by induced changes in the levels of income in the two nations. In this context, sensitivity and elasticities must all be computed between two end-of-period positions or short-run equilibria. The position of the offer curve is intimately connected with the length of the time-horizon of the analytic framework.[5]

The changing composition of import and export shares of different industries that accompany a movement along an offer curve recalls Edgeworth's famous observation about the (literal) superficiality of offer-curve analysis.[6] The description of a movement along an offer curve, from *B* to *C*, is made again with the aid of exhibits 5-1 and 5-2 and these exhibits also serve to indicate the impact upon the mix of goods traded when an industry-specific disturbance occurs.

Exhibit 5-1 shows a simplified ranking of goods by competitiveness for a trading nation. The values of r^* denote the position of the dividing line corresponding to the points on curve *OG* in figure 5-1 identified by the subscripts. The type of good is also given. Non-competitive goods and differentiated goods have been ranked by their volume of trade at *B*. Exports identified as type 1*A* are defined in terms of their characteristics in the importing nation. The ranking of goods serves

[5] See R. F. Kahn, 'Tariffs and the Terms of Trade', *Review of Economic Studies* 16, (1947—48), pp. 14—19.

[6] See F. Y. Edgeworth, 'The Theory of International Values II', *Economic Journal* 4, (September 1894), pp. 424—5: 'A movement along a supply-and-demand curve of international trade should be considered as attended with rearrangements of internal trade; as the movement of a hand of a clock corresponds to considerable unseen movements of the machinery'.

Good one	(1*A*)
Good two	(1*A*)
Good three	(3)
Good four	(3)
Good five	(3)
Good six	(2)
Good seven	(2)

r_C^*

Good eight	(2)
Good nine	(2)
Good ten	(2)

r_B^*

Good eleven	(3)
Good twelve	(3)

r_A^*

Good thirteen	(1*A*)
Good fourteen	(1*A*)

EXHIBIT 5-1

Competitiveness-ranking of Goods

merely to distinguish, in the absence of costs of transportation, between goods which are exported and those which are imported. No information is given about the volume of trade in the different goods (with the obvious exception of the ranking of non-competitive and differentiated goods). Nor is there any implication that domestic production of an individual good below the dividing line is zero. Whether consumption of an imported good is met wholly by imports depends upon the elasticities of foreign and domestic supply. Equally, when the terms of trade are quite adverse, there is no evidence for supposing that all goods above the dividing line are, in fact, exported.

Exhibit 5-2 shows the value of international trade in individual goods. It is a more complex version of exhibit 5-1. The first bar diagram (2-1) shows the mix of exports and imports by value at point *B* (in figure 5-1). The value of trade in a particular good is shown by the height of its segment. The dividing line, $r^*{}_B$, is situated at the mid-point of the bar indicating balanced trade. The absence of good 11 denotes that imports of that differentiated good were zero. The second bar diagram (2-2) shows the mix of exports and imports at point *C* on *OG* (in figure 5-1). The movement from *B* to *C* has resulted

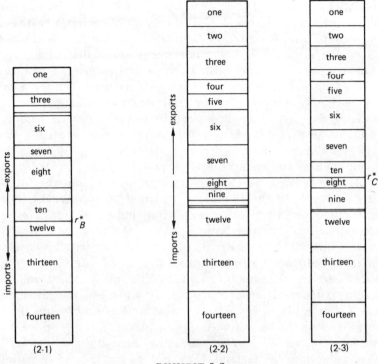

EXHIBIT 5-2

Schematic Representation of the Trade Pattern

from a general disturbance in the trading-partner nation with no induced shift in *OG*. The value of exports and imports is larger but because of the differing sensitivities of individual goods the traded values of those goods do not increase in accordance with any set pattern. Thus, the benefits to different industries from the change in international trading conditions is uneven. Presumably, those goods which switch from import-substitutes to exports benefit the most if only because of the negative effect which import competition can have upon profitability.[7] The third bar diagram (2-3) shows the trading pattern at *C* after an industry-specific disturbance in the focus country has caused

[7] See Louis and Frances Ferguson Esposito, 'Foreign Competition and Domestic Industry Profitability', *Review of Economics and Statistics* LIII, (November 1971), pp. 343–53.

the offer curve to shift. A comparison between the export and import mixes in (2-1) and (2-3) shows what has resulted from a movement from B on OG to C on OS. To make the comparison more direct, the disturbance is assumed to let the volume and value of trade be identical after both the general and the specific disturbances. Bar diagram (2-3) is therefore the same size as bar diagram (2-2). The contrast of the trading patterns reflects the difference in effect between a general and an industry-specific disturbance. The industry-specific disturbance has two dimensions: a decrease in demand for good 14 in the focus country and an increase in productivity in good 10. One of these dimensions would by itself improve and the other deteriorate the terms of trade, r^*_C. Good 10 is now an export and competes with other exporting industries for a given amount of foreign purchasing power (at the going terms of trade). Imports of goods 8, 9, 11, 12 and 13 have all increased to the detriment of the profitability of any competing industries in the focus country. The profitability in the trading-partner nation of industries 10 and 14 will be impaired. The profitability of industry 7 in the focus country would have suffered had the reduction in import demand for good 14 not been accompanied by an increase in productivity in industry 10. The reduction in demand for good 14 in the focus nation would, by itself, have improved the terms of trade and transformed good 7 from an export industry into an import-competing industry.

The multi-commodity offer curve can respond to a disturbance by changing its shape, its position or both. The difference between a general and an industry-specific disturbance is that the former will shift the curve and the latter will change its shape. The effect of an industry-specific disturbance is, by definition, concentrated upon certain individual goods (or an individual good). The more intramarginal the goods affected by an industry-specific disturbance the greater the portion of the offer curve which is liable to a change in shape. In the same way, the more a given disturbance concentrates its effects, the greater the change in shape is likely to be so that a decrease in demand for one good replaced by an equal increase in demand for a second good will have a larger proportionate effect upon the shape of the curve than will a decrease in demand for one good matched by a general increase in demand for all other goods. As was inferred above,[8] the distinction between the effect on an offer curve of a general and an industry-specific disturbance is overdrawn. Given that not all industries have linear and homogeneous production functions or that some goods have 'perverse factor intensities', a change in the supply of a generic factor will change the ranking of goods by competitiveness. Different goods will be affected differently even by a general disturbance and this will cause the shape of the offer curve to change at the same time that it shifts. Nontheless, the distinction has analytic value. An industry-specific disturbance will cause a much larger change in shape relative to the shift of the offer curve than will a general disturbance and is much more likely to have serious repercussions upon the profitability and growth of an individual industry.

To this point the offer curve has been represented as having the traditional shape. This smoothly rising curve derives from the combination of diminishing marginal rates of substitution of imports for exportables and from the existence of increasing opportunity costs in both countries. Consider again the concept of the sensitivity of international trade in a particular good to changes in the terms or trade. Sensitivity was defined above as the change in the volume of trade per unit change in the terms of trade — in the case of a change in the direction of a flow, the decrease in exports (imports) and the increase in imports (exports) are additive. There is no reason why the sensitivity of goods should, in the absence of identical linear and homogeneous production functions, be the same for all goods nor is there any reason to expect sensitivity to have any predetermined relationship with the rank ordering by competitiveness. Thus, a change in the terms of trade may induce trade in a good of greater sensitivity than the average of goods traded at less or more favourable terms of trade and the offer curve will no longer be a smooth curve; instead there will be something

[8] p. 80. Note that a general disturbance will allow analysis of the balance-of-payments adjustment process in terms of composite goods and all that is necessary for a new balance is that tradeable goods change their prices relative to domestic goods. For an industry-specific disturbance, the relative prices of tradeable goods must change: see Joseph T. Salerno, 'The International Adjustment Process: An Austrian View', Symposium on Austrian Economics, Hartford, Conn., June 22–28, 1975 for an assessment of the emphasis attributed to this phenomenon by the Austrian writers.

reminiscent of 'steps' although the curve will rise throughout its length.

As the movement takes place along an offer curve (as a result of general shifts in the foreign offer curve), the mix of exports and imports changes and so, at the same time, does the weighted sensitivity of exports and imports to the terms of trade. In the extreme case in which some exports and imports were both infinitely sensitive − supply in both countries being perfectly elastic − the slope of the offer curve would correspond to a ray from the origin and would be straight for some finite distance. The extreme case is therefore reminiscent of Graham. Any such straight segments would be minuscule and of short duration because of the existence of capacity limitations in the short-run and because of the effect of increasing opportunity costs upon competitiveness. Consider the dividing line to be quite low in the competitiveness ranking of goods, indicating relatively adverse terms of trade for the focus country and corresponding to point *B*. *B* must be 'north-east' of *A* but *AB* need not be steeper than *OA*. If the goods newly involved in trade in the segment *AB* are very sensitive to the terms of trade, the segment will be flatter than if the goods were relatively unsensitive, and if the marginal sensitivity exceeded the average, *AB* will be flatter than *OA*.

The introduction of goods with high (greater than average) sensitivity is shown in figure 5-2. The offer curve has the traditional shape in the early stages. As the terms of trade improve for the focus country, its exports will begin to displace more sensitive import-substitutes in the trading partner. Further, as manufacturing goods with high elasticities and very small differences in competitiveness are traded in both directions, sensitivities will tend to be quite high. Once the terms of trade have shifted to the point that (type 2) manufactured items are only traded in one direction, the offer curve will become more steeply sloped again. The range of high-sensitivity international trade will also include that range of the terms of trade in which differentiated goods are simultaneously both exported and imported.[9] In figure 5-2, the terms of trade are so

[9] Trade in differentiated goods in analysed in chapter 11. In the ranking of goods by international competitiveness, differentiated goods are at the extreme ends of the ranking together with type 1 goods. Of course the demand for imports of differentiated goods is very sensitive to the price of the domestically produced competing goods since the concept of a group is logically determined by the size of cross elasticities of demand.

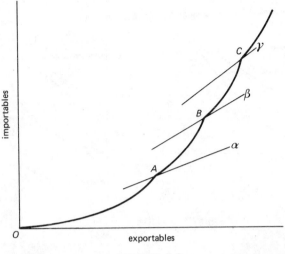

FIGURE 5-2

A Multi-commodity Offer Curve (with goods of differing sensitivities)

adverse up to point *A* that the trading partner only imports type 1 imports and the offer curve has the traditional shape. At terms of trade *OA*, foreign demand increases to the point that production abroad of highly elastic goods is displaced by exports (also highly elastic) from the focus country. The marginal sensitivity at that point is greater than average and the offer curve becomes discontinuously differentiable. However, the line is not straight because of short-run capacity limitations and the sensitivity of demand for *all* traded goods to the change in the terms of trade. As the terms of trade improve, changes in opportunity cost reduce the supply elasticity of the product and the offer curve has the traditional shape between points *A* and *B*. At the terms of trade *OB*, another highly elastic good is displaced from production in the trading partner and the offer curves 'kinks' again. The difference between the terms of trade at which successive 'kinks' take place depends upon the closeness of money costs of production (and therefore of competitiveness) of goods in the competitiveness ranking. The inference drawn above that type 2 manufactured goods and differentiated manufactures will have quite close money costs of production relies essentially upon the belief that costs among manufactures will be relatively constant in comparison with

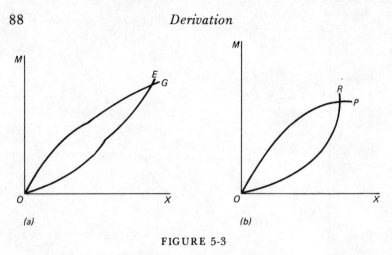

FIGURE 5-3

Different Offer Curve Relationships

primary products. The closer are these money costs, the greater the range over which the offer curve will have high elasticity (other than at the origin).[10] Thus, the offer curve of a developed or manufacturing nation such as the United States, will have one significant kink in it and the United States' trading equilibrium will be something approaching the scheme portrayed in figure 5-3(*a*). Other manufacturing nations will have similar shaped offer curves so that the equilibrium point with the rest of the world will be in the highly elastic ranges of the two offer curves despite the existence of some preceding segments of lesser elasticities. On the other hand, when the rich and the poor nations of the world are grouped in blocs, both curves will have the traditional shape since the intersection will take place before the offer curve of the developed world reaches its 'kink' (see figure 5-3(*b*)). Such a relationship supports the observation that the Heckscher—Ohlin model with its emphasis on factor proportions is more suited to analysis of trade between rich nations and poor nations than for the analysis of a manufacturing nation with the rest of the world.[11]

Figure 5-2 can be exaggerated into figure 5-4. In the latter figure the terms of trade are fixed by real factors for a relatively

[10] For a discussion of the concept of the elasticity of an offer curve see the appendix to this chapter: the Marshallian measure is used here.

[11] Note the implications for these results of S. B. Linder's dichotomy, see pp. 120—1.

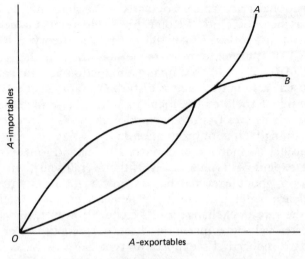

FIGURE 5-4

Assumptions Underlying the Monetarist Theory of the Balance of Payments

sizeable range of international trade. Such a state of affairs would exist when marginal and domestic foreign goods were perfectly substitutable for each other in both countries and could apply to the major industrial countries' trade with each other. This concept underlies the thinking of those proposing a monetary theory of the balance of payments in which devaluation will, in due course, produce a matching inflation of domestic prices.[12] The problem with such a concept is that the analysis is long-run equilibrium and therefore of dubious relevance to the short-run pragmatic context of international payments adjustment. Second, the monetary analysis ignores the income effects that would result from a change in the pattern of international trade.

It is possible for a change in the shape of an offer curve to bring about a severe change in the distribution of gains from

[12] See Harry G. Johnson, 'Problems of Stabilization Policy in an Integrated World Economy' in Herbert Giersch, (ed.), *Demand Management Globalsteuerung Symposium, 1971* , (Tubingen: Institut für Weltwirtschaft an der Universität Kiel, 1972), reprinted as 'The Theory of the Balance of Payments' in R. E. Baldwin and J. David Richardson, *International Trade and Finance: Readings*, (Boston: Little, Brown and Company, 1974), pp. 406–10. Also see Harry G. Johnson, 'The Monetary Approach to Balance-of-Payments Theory', *Economic Notes* I, (No. 1, 1972), pp. 20–39.

international trade and particularly those gains that derive from the payment of rental income by residents of one country to residents of another. Under the generalized theory, it is possible that what appears to be a favourable shift in the net barter terms of trade could accompany a reduction in gain from trade. The usual assumption that a disturbance abroad that improves the terms of trade of the focus nation will also increase its gain from trade derives from the orthodox theory's failure to include rent-earning factors of production.[13]

Consider an increase in country *B*'s demand for type 2 goods at the expense of type 3 goods. If the overall sensitivity to price of type 2 goods exceeds that of type 3 goods, country *B* will experience a net increase in its demand for imports. This will shift the rate of exchange in *A*'s favour. However, the change in *B*'s tastes will have increased *A*'s exports of type 2 goods and will have reduced *A*'s exports of type 3 goods initially. After the rate of exchange has adjusted to balance trade in goods and services, there will also be reduced exports of *A*'s type 1 goods. Thus, the volume of *A*'s exports will have increased for goods that do *not* earn rent at the expense of the volume of exports of rent-earning goods. It is possible, therefore, that *A*'s overall gain from international trade will have decreased despite an apparent increase in foreign demand for its exports and an improvement in the rate of exchange. The qualitative differences can outweigh the quantitative effects.

Another consequence of the introduction into the analytic framework of goods that use rent-earning factors of production is that changes in tastes among domestically produced goods (without any apparent effect on the aggregate demand for imports) can have quite serious implications for the rate of exchange and the terms of trade. A change in the domestic pattern in *A* from its type 2 export to its type 1 export will increase the rent earned by the natural resources (or other specific input) used in the production of its type 1 export, possibly by a substantial amount. The more inelastic the foreign demand for and domestic supply of *A*'s type 1 export, the greater will the increase be in *A*'s gain from trade.

[13] See Jacob Viner, *Studies in the Theory of International Trade*, (New York: Harper, 1937), pp. 555−8 for a review of this question. Most variations involve the inadequacy of the concept of net barter terms of trade and the argument introduced here is not considered by Viner.

DERIVED DISTURBANCES

The reaction of the international economic system to a disturbance must take some starting point as a datum. In this chapter, that starting point is a position in which international trade is taking place and which has achieved, at the end of the relevant period, a short-run equilibrium. There is no guarantee that the equilibrium reached within a single period is in any sense a permanent equilibrium. From such a starting point, there are two sorts of disturbances which may impinge upon the system and which, in the modern complex world, are inevitable. While such disturbances may occur simultaneously, analysis is made easier if they are deemed to occur singly. The two kinds of disturbances are (a) derived disturbances and (b) autonomous disturbances. Autonomous disturbances are those which occur without reference to the variables included in the analytic framework. They might occur as a result of changes in tastes, changes in world technology and its distribution, changes in population and discoveries of natural resources. Derived disturbances stem from discrepancies within the analysis itself between the existing short-run and the potential long-run equilibria.[14] Such discrepancies will set in motion forces that will reduce the disparities between the *status-quo* and the long-run equilibrium. Derived disturbances are, then, the consequences of events taking place in earlier periods which require, for their full impact to be felt, that factor endowments change in succeeding periods.

A derived disturbance can be most simply illustrated by reference to the familiar macroeconomic model in which changes in consumption are lagged one period behind the change in income. Looking at a sequence from the perspective of a single period, an increase in income will have been achieved in the first period in response to some autonomous disturbance. In the second period, the original increase in income features as a derived disturbance which brings about, in that same period, an increase in consumption expenditures. In an international setting a derived disturbance may follow from a disparity between the rate of return to a factor of production in two

[14] There is no suggestion that the long-run equlibrium will ever, in fact, be attained since that would imply that no autonomous disturbance would occur during the time taken for the long-run equlibrium to be achieved. (The possibility of exactly offsetting disturbances is disregarded.)

countries: in consequence of the inequality in rates of return, units of that factor will tend to move from the country with the low rate of return to that in which it would enjoy the higher rate of return. This movement would be a derived disturbance since it will take place in the shift between two succeeding periods and will bring about a change in the data in the second period.

Before examining the way in which derived disturbances will affect the structure of international trade, the starting point or existing state of affairs must be described. The simple model of the *status quo* derives from the rank ordering of goods by international competitiveness at the prevailing rate of exchange. This ranking of goods will depend upon the real variables of tastes, incomes, income-distribution, the endowments of general and industry-specific factors of production in the two nations and on the production functions of the goods themselves. Because of the interaction among the various supply elasticities and demand patterns, there can be no assurance that the ranking does not differ slightly for each rate of exchange. There is some rate of exchange that, given absolute domestic price levels, will balance international trade in the short run. Ignoring the potential impediment to the international trade that transportation costs constitute, there is some dividing line in the ranking between exports and imports. By definition, goods exported are those in which the nation has a comparative advantage.

Given the patterns of demand in the two countries, the two rank orderings of goods by international competitiveness can be attributed to the elements in the production functions: relative factor endowments, scalars and modifiers. The nation will export those goods which use relatively intensively those factors of production with which the nation is relatively plentifully endowed — those factors for which the price is relatively low. In this respect, the conclusions of the generalized theory derive directly from Heckscher's original essay. By using factor prices as the determinant of relative plentitude or scarcity, the derived effect of demand upon the mix of output is included in the mechanism by which comparative advantage is determined — explicit mention of the possibility of 'perverse tastes' or 'taste-compensated factor endowments' is no longer necessary. Probably autarkic factor price will determine relative plentitude or scarcity but there is always the possibility that the existence of international trade will so affect factor prices that autarkic prices will not be a reliable guide when the full trade exists. Further, the existence of a minimum of five factors of production implies that the determination of comparative advantage depends upon the mix of inputs as well as upon factor prices. The price of the ith good is determined by factor prices and productivity in the different goods. Using the subscripts, k, l, h, r and p to denote, respectively, physical capital, labour, human capital, natural resources and proprietary knowledge, the price of the ith good is:

$$p_i = a_{ik} \cdot p_k + a_{il} \cdot p_l + a_{ih} \cdot p_h + a_{ir} \cdot p_r + a_{ip} \cdot p_p$$

$$(5\text{-}1)$$

The role of tastes is include in the theory by the price of the factors which also subsumes the role of the production function (through the technical or input coefficients – the a_i) and factor endowments.

In a two-country model, the importance of an individual factor (j) in determining whether or not a nation has a comparative advantage in good i depends upon the size of a_{ij} in both nations and upon the differences between p_j in the two countries. This complexity explains why the capital/labour ratio will not dominate the pattern of international trade. The importance of the k/l ratio will depend directly upon the international differences in the prices of the two factors, upon the price differences of the other factors and upon the importance of capital and labour as inputs. This perspective shows why trade between two nations in similar stages of development is likely to show quite large sensitivities to the rate of exchange for many of the individual goods traded and why trade between developed and less-developed nations is more easily explained by the orthodox model.

To define the plentitude of scarcity of a factor endowment, the price of the factor must be compared to that of a generic factor that is available in both countries. Thus, a nation is well endowed with capital if the ratio of the price of (pure or generic) capital to unskilled labour is lower in that country than in its trading partner. (The elimination of the conditions needed for factor price equalization makes this approach feasible.)

The existence of industry-specific inputs affects the rank ordering of goods directly. The relative availability of such factors and their prices can overwhelm any differences between the prices of cooperating factors of production so that a good can be exported even though it may have an apparently perverse mix of the generic factors. The existence of scalars and modifiers also affects the ranking of goods by international competitiveness quite directly since a scalar will enable a nation to achieve quite low costs if there is sufficient demand. The role of the scalars in individual goods is complex since a scale-induced comparative advantage will only fail to be reversed if the foreign market never achieves sufficient domestic demand to warrant the establishment of an optimally sized plant or if scale economies continue to be achieved as quantity-produced increases. Once the market in the 'disadvantaged' country is large enough to achieve the benefit of full economies of scale and a local plant is established, the good will change drastically in the ranking.[15] Modifiers can effectively make a good non-competitive because of the lack of infrastructural requirements. Once the necessary socioeconomic conditions have been attained, the effect of the modifier disappears and the location of production is determined by scale considerations and factor endowments.

This static or starting-point version of the generalized theory can usefully be compared at this juncture with Linder's model.[16] Linder divided trade into two categories of goods which derive their comparative advantage from different sources: primary products that depend upon factor endowments and manufactured goods that require adequate market demand. Linder's essay places more emphasis on demand factors than any other important treatise on international trade. The main contribution of his approach is its vital role in explaining two-way trade in the same or competing commodities among rich nations.[17] The role of adequate demand can be explained more substantially using the concepts developed in this chapter. For an industry to continue in the production of differentiated goods when two-way trade exists,

---

[15] This is one of the crucial points in Vernon's product cycle concept. See chapter 9 below.

[16] *An Essay in Trade and Transformation*, pp. 82–109.

[17] See chapter 11 below.

it must be assured of its continued ability to compete with the foreign suppliers — at least in the home market. A steady flow of new proprietary knowledge is probably seen by the executives as prerequisite to continued competitiveness. This continuous generation of industry-specific proprietary knowledge can only be accomplished by firms enjoying large sales volume since large volume is necessary for an adequate return to be made on research-and-development expenditures that yield industry-specific proprietary knowledge. In the same way, the volume of sales must also be large enough to warrant the generation of industry-specific human capital and for the embodiment of the proprietary knowledge in productive facilities. The confidence necessary for such expenditures will only be forthcoming if there is a reliable and stable minimum market. If two-way trade exists, this condition will almost necessarily imply a large domestic market.

What Linder's essay does not do is to interrelate the two separate categories of international trade. Nowhere does he indicate that the international competitiveness of manufactured exports is negatively related to the intensity of foreign demand for the focus country's primary exports (goods using natural resources). The greater the foreign demand for primary goods, the higher the rate of exchange and the smaller the proportion of manufactured goods that will be exported and the greater the competitiveness of foreign suppliers in competition with domestic producers.

A derived disturbance is one that comes into being as a result of the short-run forces that prevail at the end of a period being inconsistent with the long-run equilibrium solution. These disturbances can be either general or industry-specific. Some factor supplies will vary in response to price changes. Thus, if a short-run equlibrium indicates a higher market price for a factor than the quantity offered at the beginning of the period is compatible with, the succeeding period will show a larger factor supply. Some factors are potentially mobile between nations. Thus, the existence of different factor prices in different countries creates the possibility of international factor migration. If the disturbance is to be general it will have reference to a generic factor of production such as human capital, physical capital or (unskilled) labour. If the disturbance is industry-specific, the change in factor supplies will exclude unskilled labour but may include physical and human capital as well as proprietary knowledge. It may well be that international movements of industry-specific factor supplies are less likely to occur singly than in groups as their value in the foreign nations depends to a significant degree upon their complementarity.[18]

Once a disturbance takes place, the economic system must adjust until a new state of balance is achieved. If the disturbance is an increase in the supply of a generic factor in one period due to an increase in its rate of return achieved in the preceding period, the whole offer curve will shift and all markets will have to adjust to the new circumstances. Presumably, the earlier increase in the price of the factor will be mitigated but not eradicated. Income distribution will change in response to the change in relative factor prices and the magnitude of the shift will be important. It is possible that changes in income distribution will induce a further disturbance by way of a change of aggregate tastes but such an effect is likely to prove small relative to the original disturbance. A general disturbance is unlikely to have major effects (favourable or adverse) on any single industry. The most serious adjustment problem would occur in a nation experiencing a favourable shift in its terms of trade which completely eliminated the international competitiveness of one of its industries so that the industry were eliminated. For such an occurrence, the marginal industry would have to be operating under constant returns to scale so that it was completely vulnerable to foreign competition. While serious disruptions of this order can and do occur, they do so gradually in the real world as the new exporter has slowly to build up its capacity and the old industry will die out relatively slowly. To the extent that industries that experience constant returns to scale are likely to be manufacturing industries that compete in monopolistically or imperfectly competitive markets, the existence of a quasi-rent from proprietary knowledge and from marketing organizations will provide a buffer that will slow the process of adjustment and reduce the social costs of rapid dislocation. The impact of a general disturbance will not differ greatly from the type of disturbance analysed in the orthodox theory. The reason for

---

[18] This clearly relates to the existence of multi-national enterprise and international investment (see chapter 9 below).

this similarity is, clearly, that general disturbances are effectively confined to changes in generic factors and tastes which are such stuff as (traditional) theories are made on. The effects of the disturbances may differ in so far as some products using non-generic factors in combination with the generic factors may have apparently perverse factor proportions and a change in the shape of the offer curve may occur. This kind of complexity is likely to have relatively small impact.

An industry-specific disturbance is much more likely to have serious and unusual repercussions. A derived industry-specific disturbance may stem from a change in the supply, in one or both countries, of an industry-specific input. Because these inputs can earn rents, a change in the supply of an industry-specific input can have important repercussions upon income distribution and upon global gains from trade.

Consider the disturbance that follows from the development of a piece of proprietary knowledge as a result of research and development expenditures induced by the high rate of return potentially available to that knowledge. If the proprietary knowledge now allows the home country to develop a type 3 goods industry, to replace imports and possibly even to export the good, the repercussions from such a disturbance can be serious.[19] The degree to which the type 3 good can generate exports will depend upon the mix of cooperating factors of production and their prices in the two countries. World welfare will not be decreased but the global gains from trade will be reduced and the erstwhile exporting nation will lose quasi-rents paid by foreigners. In addition, the erstwhile exporting firm will lose orders. Depending upon the mix of generic (and specific) factors employed in that industry, the prices of other goods will change as the factor markets adjust to the disturbance. In the country in which the proprietary knowledge has been evolved, the ratio of cooperating factors used in that industry will determine the direction of change of factor prices. Real national income will increase in the innovating nation — in part from the improved terms of trade and the transfer to domestic sources of quasi-rents. The

---

[19] This rather forced example is imposed upon the analysis at this point by the fact that proprietary knowledge is deemed to be used by its owner and is not licensed to foreign firms.

short-run pattern evolved within the period will slowly undergo further derived disturbances.

The consequences of the derived disturbance described in the preceding paragraph can be explained with reference to exhibit 5-2. Consider bar (2-2) to prevail prior to the development and utilization of the piece of proprietary knowledge. A new good would be entered into the bar above r^*_C — probably good 5a since it is a type 3 good.[20] Exports of this good may be negligible but the volume of imports of the competitive differentiated good (say good 12) may be reduced substantially. The value of r^* changes and foreign demand for other exports is reduced.

AUTONOMOUS DISTURBANCES

Autonomous disturbances arrive spontaneously and without reference to any lack of compatibility between existing prices or quantities and some set of long-run equilibrium values. Autonomous disturbances can also be general or industry-specific. General disturbances can derive from changes in income and the consequent growth in demand for the whole range of products or from some change in the supply of a generic factor that is due to influences not specifically recognized by the core theory. Industry-specific disturbances affect the demand for or supply of industry-specific factors of production in one country. A change in tastes particularly a change involving type 1 or a type 3 good — concentrated in one or a few closely related goods will constitute an industry-specific disturbance. Of course, in a multi-commodity model, a change in tastes must specify both the goods for which demand is increased as well as those goods for which demand is compensatingly decreased. What matters is the relative amounts of the different factors demanded by the expanding industries and released by the declining industries. The consequent changes in relative factor prices will be capable of inducing a shift in the offer curve, a change in its shape or both. Equally, an industry-specific disturbance can stem from an autonomous change in the supply of an industry-specific factor of production. The discovery of mineral deposit and its exploitation, the lapse of a patent or a chance new invention will all bring

[20] See exhibit 5-1.

about industry-specific disturbances. A further source of industry-specific disturbances is changes in man-made rules and regulations not explicitly considered in the theory to this point: foremost among these are tariffs and non-tariff barriers and those regulations that govern the international movement of factors of production. Barriers to trade are almost inevitably industry-specific. Changes in barriers to factor movements are general if they impede or encourage the movement of generic factors and industry-specific when they impede or encourage the movement of industry-specific factors.

The repercussions from autonomous disturbances will have effects quite like those of derived disturbances. General disturbances will spread their effects over the whole range of goods produced and traded internationally. The result of a general disturbance will be seen mainly as a change in r^* or in the position of the dividing line. Industry-specific disturbances will change the ranking of goods through their effect upon the price of specific inputs and will, therefore, have quite severe potential effects upon some individual industries — in the focus country or in the trading partner nations — as well as bringing about a change in the terms of trade.[21]

THE WORKING OF THE THEORY

At the end of a period, there exists a pattern of production and consumption as well as sets of product and factors prices. These data have been attained by the operation of the economic system given the data extant at the beginning of the period. Factor prices, together with the distribution of human capital and (physical) wealth determine income distribution and, allied with individual tastes, affect the pattern of demand. In the shift between the period just ended and its successor, there may occur, simultaneously, several changes in the underlying economic data. Some of these changes will be autonomous and will derive from happenings external to the core theory and some derive from strains set up within the system itself because the system has not been able to achieve full compatibility between the patterns of output and consumption and the supply of factors. These changes cover a multitude of economic

[21] See footnote 8 above in this chapter.

phenomena from adjustments in the supply of a factor to a disequilibrium price to a change in decision-making procedures by a multi-national corporation. Any disturbance that takes place within a shift will have its effect upon the pattern of international trade that will evolve at the end of the next period. Exactly what the impact will be depends not only upon the set of economic relationships that exist but quite directly upon the character of the disturbance.

Once a specified set of disturbances has been identified as taking place within the shift it becomes conceptually possible to deduce the changes in the pattern of international trade that will take place in the succeeding period. From this, the repercussions upon income distribution can also be inferred. The object of the exercise is to identify, at least, the direction of change in international trade flows and, from this, to examine the impact of international disturbances upon the prosperity of different countries, different industries and different groups of factors.

When a general disturbance takes place, the basic rules associated with the traditional theory hold but there can be no assurance that these rules will hold when the disturbance is industry-specific. The existence, even the predominance, of industry-specific disturbances is what qualifies the traditional theory as irrelevant. Industry-specific disturbances are sufficiently common in the real world that a generalized theory must recognize their existence. Since type 1 and type 3 goods can use generic factors in perverse amounts, industry-specific disturbances preclude sweeping generalizations being drawn about the effect of international trade upon the overall demand for factors of production.

APPENDIX TO CHAPTER 5

The elasticity of an offer curve (reciprocal demand curve) is a useful descriptive measure. It is crucial in the determination of the optimum rate of protection in the neoclassical model of international trade. Unfortunately the measure of elasticity used by T. Scitovsky and J. E. Meade[1] in their treatment of the

---

[1] Scitovsky, 'A Reconsideration of the Theory of Tariffs', *Review of Economic Studies*, (Summer 1942), pp. 89–110: reprinted in H. S. Ellis and L. A. Metzler (eds.) *Readings in the Theory of International Trade*, (Philadelphia: Blakiston, 1950), pp. 358–89. Meade, *A Geometry of International Trade*, pp. 88–9.

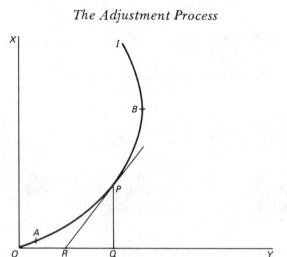

FIGURE 5-5

optimum tariff is different from that used by H. G. Johnson in his analysis of the same problem.[2] Scitovsky and Meade use Marshall's measure of elasticity (ϵ).[3] Johnson devises a new, simpler measure (η). This appendix identifies the difference between the two measures and offers a substantial reason for preferring the Marshallian measure to the Johnsonian.

In figure 5-5, OI is the offer curve of country I that exports good Y in return for imports of good X. Following Marshall, the elasticity, ϵ, is defined as:

$$\epsilon_{arc} = \frac{\Delta X}{X}\left[\frac{Y}{X} \cdot \frac{1}{\dfrac{Y}{X} - \dfrac{Y + \Delta Y}{X + \Delta X}}\right] \qquad (5\text{-}2)$$

where the expression in brackets is the reciprocal of the proportionate change in the terms of trade. In terms of figure 5-5, this expression yields a point elasticity at p of OQ/OR.

For Johnson, the definition of elasticity is:

$$\eta_{arc} = \frac{\Delta X}{\Delta Y} \cdot \frac{Y}{X} \qquad (5\text{-}3)$$

and the expression yields a point elasticity estimate of OQ/RQ.

[2] Johnson, 'Optimum Tariffs and Retaliation', in *International Trade and Economic Growth*, (London: George Allen and Unwin, 1958), pp. 31–61.

[3] Alfred Marshall, *Money, Credit and Commerce*, (London: Macmillan, 1923), Appendix J.

Thus, the fomula for the optimum tariff (t) is:

$$t = \frac{1}{\epsilon - 1} = \eta - 1 \tag{5-4}$$

Marshall's formula for elasticity is preferable because it provides an unambiguous measure. Referring to the offer curve drawn in figure 5-5, at point A, η has a value of approximately unity (it is unity if OA is a straight line). At B, η achieves a value of infinity only to turn negative immediately afterwards.[4] Marshall's formulation proceeds logically giving a value of almost infinity at A to unity at B and to less than unity but still positive beyond B.

[4] η becomes negative according to the algebraic formula. Its absolute value decreases as OI becomes progressively flatter. According to the geometric formula, η remains positive unless RQ is defined as negative when $OR > OQ$. Johnson's formula is virtually equivalent to the reciprocal of the ordinary elasticity of supply. It is this reciprocal quality which must account for its unusual quality.

6 Extensions of the Theory

The reality of the generalized theory in its development in Chapters 4 and 5 has been constrained by the several assumptions made.[1] These assumptions are also characteristic of work done with the orthodox theory. The purpose of this chapter is to release some of those assumptions so that the implications of some specified disturbance for the output-mix, income and trade structure of a nation can be analyzed under more realistic conditions. In the interests of maintaining as much simplicity as possible, the assumptions are released sequentially and not cumulatively.

The effects of the following complicating factors are examined:

1. Transportation costs
2. Imperfect competition in product markets
3. Imbalance of trade in goods and services
4. Changes in the level of aggregate demand within the two countries
5. The existence of dividend and interest payments and other unilateral transfers
6. Foreign investment — direct investment and portfolio investment

The chapter concludes with a summary assessment of the operational differences between the orthodox and generalized theories.

TRANSPORTATION COSTS

Transportation costs have two separate dimensions: the provision of the transportation services themselves and the distribution of these services by country; and the effect of transportation costs upon the volume of trade and the mix of goods traded.

[1] See pp. 56—60 above.

Transportation services are a good that uses factors of production. In this sense, transportation services are merely another item that can be traded between or among nations to mutual benefit. International transportation usually takes place in international space and is therefore not liable to the imposition of tariffs, but other means of protecting a national industry do exist. In a world free from governmental interference with international transportation, the provision of services would be allocated among nations according to the ability of nations to provide the services at the lowest money prices. Comparative advantage would be determined in the same way as for any other good — by the relative prices of different factors of production the different countries and by the mix of the factors required in the provision of the service. Since maritime and, to a lesser extent, air transportation benefit from a national tradition of service on the sea and in the air, the production functions of transportation services may have different modifiers in different nations. In practice, governments tend to subsidize their international carriers and to protect them by market-sharing agreements both because of their potential value during war and because of their value as an international prestige symbol.

Land Transportation is also important in a balance-of-payments sense but imbalances in such trade are relatively small. Land transportation by carriers of one nation within another nation's boundaries are essentially intranational transportation. In the absence of reciprocity agreements, nations are likely to insist upon trans-shipment of imports to domestic carriers at national frontiers.

Transportation costs can affect the pattern and mix of international trade in commodities and services. When considering the role of transportation costs in this second aspect of transportation, it is important to realize that the costs of transporting an internationally traded commodity include such domestic costs as loading costs in the exporting country, unloading costs in the importing country, insurance, landing fees or pier charges among other items. Transportation costs will not affect all goods equally as a percentage of f.o.b. cost. Variation in costs can derive from four main sources: the need of the good for careful handling, for speed and for shipment in small lots; variation in the bulk/value ratio; variation in the geographic distance to be transported;[2] and imperfect competition in transportation markets.

Because of the potential differences in proportionate costs of transportation, the ranking of goods by comparative advantage will be altered. Moreover, some goods — notably services — are not transportable and, if these services are to be involved in international trade, the user must be brought to the country in which the service is performed. Of all the things transported, human beings incur the highest transportation costs. They require careful handling, fast shipment, have a low bulk-to-value ratio and usually need round-trip transportation. Some other goods are excluded from international trade because they are perishable and defy transportation or because of a huge bulk-to-value ratio that makes transportation prohibitive. Such goods for which the costs of international transportation exceed the differences in money costs of manufacture in the two countries are usually referred to as domestic or non-traded goods. While it is analytically easier to assume that domestic goods are never or cannot be traded internationally, it is possible for a disturbance to increase the cost differences of domestic manufacture or to reduce the costs of transportation so that some commodities will change from non-traded to traded goods.[3]

The introduction of transportation costs into the analysis complicates the ranking process of commodities by comparative advantage as was described in the derivation of exhibit 5-1. When transportation costs were assumed to be zero, relative competitiveness derived from a comparison of the domestic selling prices of the good in the two nations in which it was or might be produced. The inclusion of transportation costs means that the basis for comparison differs in the two countries and the two rankings are no longer equivalent. The basis for comparison now is the selling price of domestically produced goods in the importing country and the landed price of imports (foreign selling price f.o.b. plus transportation costs). Differences in the rates charged for different goods mean that the ranking of goods will now be different in both nations. Because

---

[2] In a two-country world recognition of geographic distance is at odds with the assumption that intranational location does not affect the pattern of trade.

[3] See I. F. Pearce, 'The Balance-of-Payments Problem', *International Economic Review* 2 (1961), pp. 1—28, for an example of this simplifying assumption.

the ranking is a function of the varying costs of transportation for different goods, a change in the level of transportation costs will affect different goods differently and is, therefore, an industry-specific disturbance. Market imperfections in international transportation — shipping conferences, for example — can, like all industries with marginal cost less than average cost, discriminate among goods (customers) and can charge what the traffic will bear. This discrimination affects not only different commodities on the same route but sometimes the same commodity on the same route in different directions and the same commodity on different, competitive routes. Monopoly powers such as these will affect the ranking of goods by comparative advantage and a change in the degree of market power will therefore be likely to generate an industry-specific disturbance. The greater the average costs of transportation per unit distance, the more sensitive is international trade in a commodity to distance.

The existence of transportation costs is responsible for the existence of non-traded goods. As a result of transportation costs an industry will not suddenly switch from an export industry to an import-substitute industry in response to a small change in the exchange rate. Given different demand patterns in different countries, domestic goods can have production functions that will lead to international trade comprising goods with seemingly perverse factor-intensities. It is also barely possible that there exists a correlation between the production functions of traded goods and the costs of transportation such that international trade will demonstrate apparently perverse factor-intensities.

If transportation costs per unit of value increase with the stage of processing of a good — a reasonable observation given the greater care in handling needed by more advanced goods and the likelihood that they will be shipped in smaller lots — transportation costs can have a similar impact on the location of an activity as can the cascading of tariffs. The greater the increase in costs of transportation as a good nears its final stage, the greater is the likelihood that the final process (and the intermediate processes) will be undertaken in the nation of final consumption.[4]

---

[4] For an analysis of the implications of cascading tariffs for the effectiveness of protection see Herbert G. Grubel, 'Effective Tariff Protection: A Non-Specialist

IMPERFECT COMPETITION IN PRODUCT MARKETS

It is selling price that governs international competitiveness in world trade in a commodity. Differences in comparative advantage can be overshadowed by the pricing policies of firms in imperfectly competitive markets or by national economic policies that institute barriers to international trade. The optimum global allocation of resources is only achieved in a perfectly competitive world when selling prices are disciplined by competition among suppliers. The existence of imperfect product markets will reduce the global gain from trade.

To the extent that imperfectly competitive industries cause their internal or international selling prices to deviate from marginal costs and from what Haberler calls 'full average cost',[5] the pattern of international trade will be altered. The effect of such behaviour by an imperfect competitor will involve dumping or reverse dumping — selling abroad at a price different from the domestic sales price. The usual assumption is that the imperfect competitor will face more severe competition in foreign markets than at home and will therefore sell abroad at a price lower than his domestic price. Relative to the pattern of trade that would have existed in a perfectly competitive world and assuming the foreign demand for the good to be elastic to price (as is necessary if dumping is to take place), the value of r^* will be higher. Other export industries and import-substitute industries would be adversely affected by such behaviour. In practice, such a result would occur only when long-period dumping is being undertaken since sporadic or intermittent dumping would probably be countered by commercial policy or the dumped goods would be paid for out of foreign exchange reserves and not allowed to affect the value of the exchange rate. A higher export price would have the same effect if foreign demand were inelastic to price.

Introduction to the Theory, Policy Implications and Controversies', in Herbert G. Grubel and Harry G. Johnson, (eds.), *Effective Tariff Protection* (Geneva: General Agreement on Tariffs and Trade and Graduate Institute of International Studies, 1971), pp. 1—15.

[5] Gottfried Von Haberler, *The Theory of International Trade* (New York: The Macmillan Company, 1950), pp. 296—302.

IMBALANCE IN TRADE IN GOODS AND SERVICES

There is no need for trade in goods and services to balance in the short run. The emphasis of international trade theory on conditions of balanced trade can be attributed to the long-run general equilibrium cast of the orthodox model. Such a theory is designed to be capable of a timeless equilibrium. It must not, therefore, contain the seeds of its own destruction. A trade imbalance must, even in an otherwise stationary state, affect the international distribution of wealth between the nations over time. The trade surplus would result in a stream of dividends and interest being paid to the surplus nation and that stream would grow with the size and duration of the imbalance. The stationary model would be internally inconsistent. An imbalance of trade is a commonplace in the real world and exports and imports are under no compulsion to balance in the short run. Frequently national economic authorities impede such balancing forces as may exist and resort to the financing of deficits by borrowing from the surplus nation.[6]

Assume that the cause of the imbalance is simply that the rate of exchange actually prevailing in the foreign exchange market is not that which will balance trade or payments under the prevailing conditions (including income levels in the two countries). The failure of the foreign exchange market to establish imbalance is due to the active intervention of the authorities in the deficit nation. The situation is depicted in figure 6-1 which is taken from figure XXXVIII in Meade's *Geometry*. Assume that the deficit of country *B* is *OG*. This is drawn as a preordained sum rather than as a consequence of the support of the authorities and *OB* is drawn under the assumption that the deficit of *OG* will be incurred. The rate of exchange is *GQ*. These terms of trade are less favourable to country *A* than would exist under balanced trade and more favourable to country *B*. (The terms of trade needed for balanced trade are not shown in the figure since *OB* would have to be redrawn.) In terms of exhibit 5-2, country *A*'s export bar would be longer than its import bar. Exports will be greater

---

[6] For the purposes of this analysis, interest and dividend payments and receipts are deemed to be included in unilateral transfer account rather than in goods and services account. This approach has a good precedent — see Richard N. Cooper, 'The Competitive Position of the United States', in S. E. Harris (ed.), *The Dollar in Crisis* (New York: Harcourt Brace Inc., 1961), pp. 137–64.

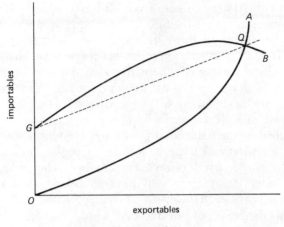

FIGURE 6-1

Unbalanced Trade in Commodities

(the offer curves have been drawn with the orthodox shape for simplicity)

than would prevail under balanced trade and, presumably, imports will be less. As a consequence, the output of both types of tradeable good will exceed that which would be achieved under balanced trade. The division of the overall increase in the output of tradeable goods will be distributed among the individual goods according to their sensitivities to the rate of exchange.

The undervaluation of the focus country's currency is the cause of the postulated trade imbalance. Provided that the trade imbalance is only of short duration, the tradeable-goods industries are unlikely to base long-run capacity decisions on the transitory increases in demand. But, if the trade surplus lasts for some length of time, the tradeable-goods industries can plan for capacity additions whose desirability will disappear once the trade surplus is eliminated. A trade surplus due to an undervaluation of a currency must ultimately disappear. In this way a protracted trade surplus (or deficit) can lead to a misallocation of investment among industries. Such a misallocation would aggravate the adjustment problem.[7] There is a built-in bias that will make the misallocation potentially more wasteful; those

[7] This hypothesis was first outlined in Nicholas Kaldor, 'Conflicts in National Economic Objectives', *The Economic Journal* LXXXI (March 1971), pp. 1–16.

industries most likely to plan for additional capacity because of the decreased competitiveness of foreign suppliers in either market will tend to be those industries for whom the increase in demand is the greatest. These industries will be those whose products show the greatest sensitivity to the rate of exchange. When the undervaluation of the currency is removed, these industries are destined to be those whose foreign competition will increase most severely.

A surplus on the balance of goods and services is the one way in which a nation can hope to add to aggregate demand for its own factors of production. Presumably, the demand for relatively plentiful factors will have increased as a result of international trade. However, a trade surplus will generate additional demand for all factors. Those factors which will enjoy the greatest relative increases in demand are those which are used intensively in goods with the greatest sensitivity to the rate of exchange.

If a nation has balance on goods and services account and a single predominant export, the potential growth of domestic industries producing other tradeable goods will be impaired. It makes no difference whether the dominance of the individual export is due to a strong comparative advantage in that one good or due to an export cartel that recognizes the inelasticity of foreign demand. If one industry dominates exports, the rate of exchange will be high and other tradeable-goods industries will suffer from severe foreign competition. The development of viable import-substitute industries can only take place if the rate of exchange (r^*) is lowered. This would require planned acquisition of foreign assets and a matching export surplus. The more sensitive is the trade balance to a change in the rate of exchange, the larger will be the foreign investment required to effect a given shift in r^*. Such dominance is likely only to occur for an export that is a type 1 import for the importing nation. Probably such an export would earn rent which may offset the social cost of the impediment to the development of the import-substitute industries. For a developing nation, the importation of its own type 1 goods and spending the rent on capital formation will prevent the exchange rate from being too high and will allow the development of import-substitute industries to some degree.

CHANGES IN THE LEVEL OF AGGREGATE DEMAND
WITHIN THE TWO COUNTRIES

Even under stationary conditions, the composition of international trade and the value of r^* will be sensitive to variation in the level of aggregate demand in the two nations. The theory of international trade in so far as it concerns the volume and mix of goods traded has not concerned itself very greatly with changes in demand other than in a growth context. Changes in demand have usually been applied in international economics to the transfer problem under the so-called Keynesian assumptions and, to a lesser degree, to the absorption approach to balance-of-payments adjustments.[8] Both of these approaches are essentially aggregative in the sense of either being conducted purely in terms of import/income relationships or in two-commodity models.

Changes in the level of aggregate demand cannot avoid having compositional effects and these compositional effects will be transmitted to the international trade sector. To this point the concept of sensitivity has been defined in terms of proportionate changes in the volume of exports or imports to a proportionate or given change in the rate of exchange. Full employment was assumed to prevail in both countries. The concept of sensitivity is equally applicable to changes in the level of income or absorption. The income-sensitivity of goods involved in international trade will be determined largely by income-elasticities of demand and output-elasticities of supply in the short run. Any concomitant price changes would also influence income-sensitivity.

When the level of aggregate demand in a nation exceeds productive capacity, the volume of imports tends to expand rapidly. The composition of the increased volume of imports will depend upon the composition by commodity or service of the increase in aggregate demand as well as upon the income-sensitivity of those commodities. If foreign supplies are perfectly elastic and foreign spare capacity exists and the deficit is financed so that r^* is not changed, the composition of the excess demand will all spill over into imports. Foreign supply

---

[8] See Harry G. Johnson, 'The Transfer Problem and Exchange Stability' in *International Trade and Economic Growth*.

conditions will affect the composition of the spill-over. Probably manufactured items are the most sensitive to levels of domestic capacity utilization.[9]

When aggregate demand falls below full employment levels in either or both nations, the composition of international trade will again change. Increases in the availability of certain exports may give them small negative sensitivity to a decline in domestic aggregate demand but imports and other exports will be likely to have large and positive income-sensitivities. Differentiated goods will be likely to have particularly high sensitivity in that they may have high income elasticities of demand. In the short run, factor substitution is limited and money wages tend to be sticky downwards. Thus, the effect of international trade on income by factor shares will, in times of deficient aggregate demand, depend very much upon the new composition of international trade. Changes in trade volume of different goods and the relative factor inputs into those goods will determine the effect of deficient demand on income by factor shares in the short run.

A sharp change in the composition of total demand in a nation can also result in a sudden change in the pattern of international trade. A change in the mix of goods demanded may not be capable of being met by the productive sector without a prolonged period of investment. The disparity between domestic demand and supply will be met by imports. This phenomenon may show itself as an increase in aggregate demand despite the fact that aggregate absorption may be more or less constant — what has happened is not so much that absorption has increased, more that income or output defined in terms of the pattern of demand has decreased. Such an increase in imports will last only until the domestic capacity has adapted itself to the changed pattern of demand. During the period of adjustment, the ranking of goods by comparative advantage may change substantially and may be temporarily different from the ranking that would prevail in the long run, given factor endowments and the (new) tastes of the nation.

---

[9] See John J. Arena, 'U.S. Imports and the Manufacturing Utilization Rate', *New England Business Review* (August 1967), pp. 3–7.

THE EXISTENCE OF DIVIDEND AND INTEREST PAYMENTS
AND OTHER UNILATERAL TRANSFERS

The existence of international transfers has the main effect of making an imbalance on goods and services capable of existing in perpetuity. Other than that effect, the impact of a constant flow of interest and dividends and of unilateral transfers can be analyzed together with international investment since all categories are 'transfers' rather than payments for current goods and services. Interest and dividends derive from foreign assets and are therefore likely to be payable or receivable for long periods of time. There are sources of fluctuation in the flow but these sources are usually closely allied to variations in income levels and can be analyzed as a part of business cycles in international trade. Growth in asset holdings over time will also affect the net flow of dividends and interest. The potential of such flows (unless offset by capital flows) for employment can be quite severe. Lawrence B. Krause has pointed out the implications of increased flows of dividends and interest for the 'balance of labour' from international trade for the US economy. As interest and dividend receipts increase, the volume of net exports will gradually be eroded and employment levels in the more sensitive industries will suffer.[10] It is, perhaps, part of the natural perversity that seems to dominate economic matters that net creditors whose employment levels are likely to be damaged are indeed those affluent nations that can, from time to time, suffer serious inadequacies of aggregate demand.

There is one type of transfer payment that deserves particular attention since it can embody a pure or quasi-rent. This is the return on the licensing of proprietary knowledge by the owner of the knowledge in one nation to a user in a second nation. Licensing fees and royalties are often earned when exporting the knowledge embodied in goods is not feasible and when foreign direct investment is not considered worthwhile. Just as receipts of dividends and interest can erode the value of net exports, so too can the licensing of knowledge reduce the balance on goods and services. To the extent that either of these flows actually do reduce net exports, then the benefits that

---

[10] 'Trade Policy for the Seventies', *Columbia Journal of World Business* 6 (January—February 1971), pp. 5—14. In this article Krause also conceives of different sensitivities to the rate of exchange but does not develop the concept.

derive to the relatively plentiful factors from international trade are also reduced.

Unilateral transfers, including licensing fees, dividends and interest, have their effect upon the pattern of national demand and, through that, upon the demand for and availability of internationally traded goods in world markets. The major implication of a net inflow of interest and dividends is to increase the importance of the business sector and of stock-holders' tastes in the determination of the overall pattern of demand. On the other hand, payment of government-to-government aid will enhance the demand for exports of certain types of goods by recipient governments. Exactly how the demand for exports will be affected is not easy to deduce but aid payments to poor nations are likely to engender added demand for manufactured exports — particularly for capital goods and armaments.

The demand for a country's exports is determined by the relationship between its trading partners' tastes and their income. Dividend and interest payments will reduce the national equivalent of 'discretionary income' or discretionary foreign exchange for some nations more than others. Thus, the pattern of geographic receipts of dividends and interest will also affect the pattern of demand for exports and through that the value of r^*.

FOREIGN INVESTMENT — DIRECT INVESTMENT AND PORTFOLIO INVESTMENT

Net transfers of capital that are made for their own inherent desirability (autonomous investments) permit a current-account surplus to exist for an extended period of time. They also generate return flows of dividends and interest which will slowly offset the net transfer of a constant outflow of capital. Thus, the effect of foreign investment on the pattern of international trade has already been analyzed under the topics of a current-account imbalance and net receipts of dividends interest. But the more distinctive feature of foreign investment — particularly direct investment — is that it will alter the potential pattern of effective demand in the two nations. For the pattern of global demand to differ, the tastes of the investors (savers) must be different from the tastes of the spenders in terms of exports and imports from the respective countries of residence. Portfolio investment will ordinarily have only a general-disturbance effect on demand. Direct investment will be much more likely to have an identifiable, industry-specific effect. The process of direct investment, defined as the flow of capital rather than as the volume of foreign-owned assets, will usually lead to the increase of the host nation's imports of capital goods during the current period as a result of the capital inflow. In a multi-country model, there is a high probability that the investing nation will, itself, be the supplier of the capital goods. In later periods, once the subsidiary or the expansion of capacity, has become productive, exports of finished goods from the investing country to the host country may have been reduced and exports of intermediate or semi-finished goods may have increased. [11] Since these flows of traded goods pertain directly to the industry engaged in the international investment process, the disturbance is industry-specific.

There is no reason to suppose that the flows of commodities that are induced by the establishment of foreign (manufacturing) subsidiaries will run counter to the true pattern of comparative advantage. The mere fact that international trade can take place at other than arm's length and among subsidiaries of the same parent, need not imply that the trade pattern will be non-rational. Indeed, multi-national corporations may, by virtue of their better communications network, be able to obey the precepts of comparative advantage more thoroughly and exactly than groups of independent firms. It is possible that a network of subsidiaries basing its decisions upon private marginal costs may pervert comparative advantage as a result of tax factors or similar phenomena.

The main effect of imbalanced trade in goods and services — made possible by deficit financing, by net transfers of dividends and interest or by net international investment flows — is to re-emphasize the role of demand in international trade. Both the orthodox and the generalized theories of international trade emphasize differences in factor endowments as the main source of comparative advantage. This is probably a

---

[11] See *An Aggregate Theory of International Payments Adjustment* (London: Macmillan, 1974) pp. 131–49.

correct emphasis given that factor endowments are capable of much greater variation than are tastes. The orthodox theory has very little to say about the role of demand. The generalized theory, by relying explicitly upon the prices of factors of production and of goods to determine comparative plentifulness and advantage, does attribute an important role to demand since the derived demand for the factor of production is crucial to its ultimate price — but even this allowance for demand factors is 'passive'. However, the existence of imbalanced trade makes any consequent change in the pattern of trade directly attributable to the redistribution of purchasing power, and, through that, to demand factors. Note that the redistribution of purchasing power will amount to a series of small industry-specific disturbances since demand pattern will be affected primarily by the income elasticities of demand of the gainers and the losers. These effects will be mitigated by any induced change in the rate of exchange which will operate through price elasticities. The potential effect of direct investment on the pattern of trade through its impact on the pattern of demand is reinforced by its industry-specific nature that allows the capital transfers to flow in both directions simultaneously. The quantitative effect on the demand pattern will reflect the gross flows rather than the net flows.

Dividends and interest payments can flow in both directions simultaneously. These flows can, when the consequence of direct investment, result in the transfer of rents and quasi-rents. In this way, they can have a disproportionately large effect on the redistribution of purchasing power and through that on the role of tastes on the pattern of trade.

CONCLUSION

The generalized theory attributes the pattern and the general mechanism of international trade to differences in taste-compensated factor endowments. Its basic form is, therefore, largely a development of Eli Heckscher's original classic essay. In its multiplicity of goods and factors, the generalized theory is also faithful to the spirit of Heckscher in that article. The explicit distinguishing of non-competitive and differentiated goods and the explicit recognition of proprietary knowledge and human capital broaden Heckscher's original frame of reference into a theoretical framework that can be applied to a wide range of real-world analytic problems. The narrow applicability of the orthodox theory is one of the causes of its unsatisfactoriness and its rejection. The generalized theory is less susceptible to mathematical manipulation directly because of the features that provide it with broader applicability. The emphasis on the short run, in particular, permits the generalized theory to escape from the straitjacket of concern only with balanced trade and current goods and services. But, once the assumption of balanced trade is released, the difficulties of useful mathematical manipulation are greatly enhanced.

In the course of its development, the generalized theory uncovered some fundamental weaknesses in the orthodox model. These weaknesses consist primarily of the effects of introducing multiple goods and factors. The inherent criticisms, then, imply the lack of relevance of conclusions of the orthodox theory for the real world rather than any internal inconsistency in the orthodox theory itself. These flaws can be summarized at this point.

The orthodox theory, by ignoring international trade in non-competitive goods (types $1A$ and $1C$) seriously under-estimates global gains from trade. This is certainly true for the transition from autarky to full trade and is very probably true for the loss that would accompany a reversion from full trade to autarky. The underestimate has two roots. Most important is the availability of particular goods only through the process of international trade. Clearly such goods could seriously curtail the ability of a nation to make use of or to produce technological gains. Thus, the absence of steel in a nation without iron ore would cripple the whole technological base of the economy. The second aspect is the failure to recognize the possibility that rents paid by foreigners can flow in two directions simultaneously. Rents represent gains from international trade that far exceed those made from the exchange of competitive homogeneous goods.

Reciprocal demand curves deserve the epithet 'reciprocal' more thoroughly than the classical economists realized. The offer curve involves not only the measurement of the reciprocation of imports demanded for exports renounced but the offer curves of the two nations reciprocate in the sense that a disturbance in one country can cause a shift in the trading

partner's offer curve as well. This interdependence derives from
the fact that the change in the output mix in the focus country
as the terms of trade change, depends upon the various
income-and price-elasticities of demand and output in the two
countries concerned. The offer curve of a nation must be a
series of intersections with the offer curve of the rest of the
world. The series of intersections implies a shifting foreign offer
curve and these shifts can affect the shape and position of the
focus-country curve. A national offer curve is therefore not
unique and must be recognized as a simplification useful mainly
for exposition or in highly aggregative analyses.

Reciprocal demand curves may also be 'kinked' in a manner
reminiscent of the Graham–Elliott construct. This kinking can
be important in explaining the relative constancy of the
exchange rate between countries in the face of disturbances and
in incorporating Linder's ideas into the main body of international trade theory.

There is a legitimate question as to whether the generalized
theory is, in some strict sense, scientific. If the criterion for a
scientific statement is that the statement be Popper-refutable,
the generalized theory may not satisfy the criterion.[12] The
world, at the microeconomic level, is too complex for so strict a
criterion to be satisfied or so general a theory to be refuted.
However, the traditional theory has been refuted by Leontief
and Baldwin for the United States and by Leontief's disciples
for nearly all other countries.[13] On the other hand, the
generalized theory is Archibald-comparable in the sense that,
within the limits of econometrics and the data, the theory can
be compared with other explanations of the pattern and
structure of international trade and payments. Indeed, the
generalized theory is something of a synthesis of studies that
may be said to support its Archibald-comparability.[14]

To an important extent, the degree to which a theory lets
itself be compared with other theories does depend upon the

[12] For an excellent analysis of what constitutes theory in economics, see
G. C. Archibald, 'Refutation or Comparison?', *British Journal of Philosophical
Science* 17 (1966), pp. 279–96.

[13] See Robert E. Baldwin, 'Determinants of the Commodity Structure of U.S.
Trade', *American Economic Review* 61 (March 1971), pp. 126–46. But see Caves'
faith in the orthodox model in *Trade and Economic Structure*, p. 282.

[14] Notably in the works of Gruber, Mehta and Vernon, Keesing, Kenen, Belassa,
Grubel, Leontief and Vanek.

complexity of what the theory seeks to explain and the complexity of the theory. This is merely an alternative approach to the question raised in chapter 1 about the optimum degree of complexity of a core theory. This optimum may, legitimately, depend on personal tastes and on some abstract set of values as well as upon some impersonal criterion of demarcation between scientific and metaphysical thinking. Nor is there any reason why the optimum need remain constant through time since it will be subject to definition in terms of the state of the world's problems that exist and in terms of the technical knowhow and data-base that economic science incorporates at any given time.

Part Two
Application

Introduction to Part Two

The purpose of Part Two is to apply the theoretical construct developed in Part One to some important aspects of international economic behaviour that have not been satisfactorily dealt with by the orthodox theory. The list of applications is not, and cannot be, exhaustive.

The problem of the presentation of these applications is itself a difficult one. The problems chosen are not so disparate that there is no overlap among them and a topic covered in one chapter may well have had an aspect of it developed in a preceding chapter. The inevitability of this untidiness can be shown with reference to the problem of commercial policy. It is not possible to consider the economic dimensions of colonialism without treating the subject of the legal and trading dominance of the mother country and the implications of this dominance for the pattern of trade. In the same way, direct international investment cannot be satisfactorily explained without reference to the role of tariff barriers in inducing investment to 'jump over the tariff wall' or to 'creep under the tariff curtain'. The sequence in which the individual topics are presented below, has been chosen in the interests of clarity of exposition rather than for any reasons of importance — real-world or theoretical — of the topics analyzed.

Nor does length of the individual chapters provide any information upon the importance of a subject or of the contribution of the generalized theory to a satisfactory analysis of that topic. Differences in length and depth of treatment derive, for the most part, from the degree of complexity that best suits the contribution of the generalized theory to the analysis. Since the contribution of the generalized theory can be both vital and straightforward, a chapter can be quite short even for so important a subject as human migration.

7 Colonialism

Hopes of political aggrandizement, dreams of treasure and even competitive faddism can explain the invasion and colonization of the relatively backward nations by the European powers in the seventeenth, eighteenth and nineteenth centuries. The economic reasons for colonization and attempts to colonize were often important and sometimes necessary and sufficient. Whatever the motivation behind the original action, the enduring benefit of a colony – short of some sort of despoilation or tribute – can be explained in terms of international economics. The process of colonization benefited the mother country and her expatriate nationals in three main ways – through gains from international trade between the colony and the mother country, by factor migration, and by commercial policy. Trade benefited the citizens of the developed, colonial power primarily through the ability of the colony to supply non-competitive goods to the mother country. Migration of factors permitted both industry-specific and generic mobile factors to be moved to combine with the industry-specific immobile factors located in the colonies. Commercial policy benefited the mother country (usually) by reserving for her, the primary role in determining the pattern of the colony's trade.

TRADE BETWEEN COLONY AND MOTHER COUNTRY

In early history, long-distance international trade was confined to non-competitive goods with a very high ratio of value (in the importing countries) to bulk and therefore to transportation costs (including risk of robbery and loss). Pepper and other spices were pre-eminent examples. The importation of these spices from Asia to Europe was trade in non-competitive goods since the European nations lacked both the climate and the plants to begin local cultivation. The caravans of the middle ages were succeeded by the international trading companies of the Dutch, British and French. The establishment of these companies was, perhaps, the supreme act of faith of mercantilism since the companies usually enjoyed the protection of their governments and the governments' armed forces in support of their monopsony position in the source areas and the monopoly position in the European nation.

The importance of non-competitive goods in the creation of European colonial empires was paramount. The maritime powers of Portugal and Spain were tempted by the profits of the Venetians in the spice trade and it was a direct consequence of this profitability that Christopher Columbus and Vasco da Gama sailed in search of a maritime route to the Indies in the last decade of the fifteenth century.[1] The immense profits of the Venetians were made possible by the rent that accrued to the industry-specific factors of production located in the Spice Islands. These rents only accrued to the growers in those islands when the product was brought into contact with the effective demand that existed in Europe. In this way the Venetian traders helped to create the economic rent that they reaped.

The political aspects of colonization were not necessary for the original creation of the mercantile companies in tropical areas.[2] But the establishment of the mercantile companies did require some sort of ability to establish resident representatives of the importing nation (the potential colonial power) in the foreign area or source country of the non-competitive goods. Once these buying agents were established locally, it was necessary to ensure their safety. As domestic demand for the non-competitive imports in the mother country grew and a better local knowledge of local production conditions and processes was acquired by the expatriate buyers, the desirability of introducing western methods into the production process became obvious. Thus, what might originally have been con-ceived as a trading outpost was seen to have a future that would involve the rationalization of production, the acquisition of (rent-earning) land by the trading company and the introduc-tion of large-scale operations. For any venture such as this, protection of the capital and personnel became necessary and the assumption of a political overlordship followed naturally. It was not always clear whether trade followed the flag or vice

[1] See Adam Smith, *The Wealth of Nations* II (3rd Cannan edition), (London: Methuen, 1922), pp. 60–1.
[2] For a brilliant picture of the early years of a trading relationship see Maurice Collis, *Siamese White*, (London: Faber and Faber Ltd., 1965).

versa, but it was clear that military support and local political control were necessary for the economic gains of the trading relationship to reach their potential.

It was the search for non-competitive goods in a relatively backward, underpopulated and/or tropical nation that led to the establishment of a trading relationship between the source country and the European nation. One externality deriving from the establishment of a trading relationship, whether through a national trading monopoly (such as the British East India Company) or through private enterprise, is the spread of knowledge about the potential for trade between the source-country and the manufacturing country. This knowledge and the establishment of sets of correspondence between exporting and importing agents and distributors in the two nations are vital ingredients in what may be called 'an ongoing trading relationship'. It is the ongoing trading relationship that illumi-nates the potential for international or intra-empire trade in other, additional non-competitive goods and in competitive goods. The ultimate pattern of (and gain from) trade may owe as much to the secondary force of the network of trading relationships and information as to the original cause of trade in some particular group of non-competitive goods.

The pattern of trade in non-competitive and competitive goods, in so far as it concerns exports from the manufacturing or mother country, is likely to owe a great deal to commercial policy measures imposed by the mother country. This is not to deny a role to comparative advantage and the existence of a precolonization network of trading relationships but the essence of colonialism in its early form was excessive mercantilism.

Because colonialism derives its *raison d'être* from trade in non-competitive goods and the rents that can be earned by immobile industry-specific factors, the orthodox theory has nothing useful to say about the subject.[3]

INTRA-EMPIRE FACTOR MOBILITY

However greatly the potential gains from trade in non-competitive imports may have influenced the establishment of

[3] John H. Williams, 'The Theory of International Trade Reconsidered', pp. 265–71 remarks on the failure of the classicists to distinguish adequately between domestic trade and trade between a mother country and a colony. Their theory of international trade did not encompass colonial–metropolitan relations.

the original trading relationship, and however greatly the desire to further and expand that trade may have contributed to the decision to impose political control on the source-country, the economic aspects of the process of colonization must be analyzed as a broader phenomenon than a straightforward matter of trade flows. Integral to the process of colonization and to the resulting mother country—colony economic relationship is the transfer of factors of production to the colony.

As noted above, the institution of international trade in non-competitive goods would bring to the attention of the expatriate traders an apparent lack of efficiency in the indigenous production methods. Probably the most obvious handicap to increases in local output was the scarcity of capital employed. Local production processes may well have been technically efficient given local relative factor costs (prices) but the expatriates would tend to envision a combination of capital priced at the cost prevailing in the mother country and of labour at the local rate. The ability to combine home-country capital with local labour in the production of non-competitive goods would yield a huge quasi-rent to the imported capital provided that the capital were protected against political risk.

It is the need for protection of factors of production sent to the source-country against political risk that will have provided the incentive for the imposition of political overlordship by the mother country. Only under a system of laws that recognized the property rights of mother-country nationals could the risk factor be reduced to a tolerable and profitable level.

But physical capital does not flow unaccompanied. With the flow of physical capital and trading capital, came proprietary knowledge and embodied technology. These factors, in turn, require industry-specific human capital and with the skilled technicians came the managers with their inventory of managerial knowhow from practices in the mother country. Each of these other factors also had, potentially, very large marginal products but the human beings that were destined to accompany the capital needed to be paid a large part of the quasi-rent they earned *and* they needed to be assured of physical safety. The physical safety derived from political overlordship but there was still a risk for humans (payment for which ate into the quasi-rent) in the form of exposure to diseases against which they had no inherited immunity.

By the time the colonization process had fully matured, a

large change in factor endowments had been experienced in t
source country or colony. Changes in scalars and modifiers ha
also been experienced in the production functions of tradeabl
goods and the economy of the colony had been transformed
This economic transformation was frequently very uneven anc
enclaves were created in which the exportable goods were
produced with a minimum of contact with the rest of the
colony. In Myrdal's terminology, the colonization process had
very limited 'spread effects'.

Weak spread effects notwithstanding, it might appear that the
larger output of exportable goods and the introduction of
additional capital and new technology would have increased the
source-country's gross national product. Whether it did so or
not probably depends upon the set of accounting conventions
used. If residence is the basis for the computation of GNP, the
GNP probably increased despite the normal adverse movement
of the net barter terms of trade that accompanies pro-trade
biased economic growth. But large portions of the increase in
GNP were paid to expatriates or siphoned off in the form of
profits paid to entrepreneurs in the mother country. The
increase in GNP will have accrued primarily to the owners of
those factors of production that engendered rents or quasi-
rents. These factors were predominantly owned by or embodied
in expatriates. One of the first steps in colonization was the
acquisition by mother-country nationals of the rent-earning
land. The effect of factor ownership was reinforced by the
strong monopsony position (with respect to exportable goods)
that the colonial power was able to and did impose. This will
have kept the prices of exportables low. The expatriate
population undoubtedly lived well but they spent much of
their income on attempts to reproduce life in the home country
as nearly as possible. These attempts produced a large demand
for imports into the colony from the mother country (differentiated goods, in effect). The import demand was supplemented
by the fact that savings were kept in the mother country and
the short working life of the expatriates resulted in a high
propensity to save and therefore in large transfer flows from the
colony to the mother country. All of these factors depressed
the terms of trade that were enjoyed by the indigenous
population with reference to the mother country. If GNP were
to be computed on the basis of the indigenous population

alone, purely economic gains from colonization would be quite small and possibly negative.

The Latin word, *colonia*, signifies simply a plantation.[4] The role of factor migration from the mother country to the colony can be shown by Gunnar Myrdal's study of the plantations in South Asia.[5] Not only were technology, capital and humans introduced to the non-reproducible asset of the South Asian climate but their introduction discriminated among crops according to the marginal products of the transferred factors in different types of agriculture. The development of plantations was, according to Myrdal, a process of industrialization. The most vital factor to be made available to the plantations was capital. Plantations were devoted very largely to 'wood plants' (as opposed to grasses or root crops) and large investments were required for the intensive farming that plantations undertook. In some cases as much as ten years elapsed between the clearing of the land and the first returns. Such a period of gestation was beyond the scope of traditional agriculture. The more intensive farming also meant reliance upon wage labour with all the consequent need for scheduling, money payments and medical care. Myrdal quotes a Ceylon planter to the effect that 'tea estates are highly organized pieces of machinery which cannot function without efficient management and a permanent labour force'.[6] The managerial skills were also needed because of the large-scale of the undertaking that was made possible only by a predominantly export market and with advanced shipping—marketing—transportation arrangements.

There is no reason to presume that the non-agricultural extractive activities that comprise the other main category of non-competitive imports did not follow the pattern set by the plantations. Enclave mining industries successfully used capital-intensive techniques to achieve economies of large-scale production and to increase the flow of minerals. The success of these industries was the result of a marriage between western or metropolitan knowhow and indigenous factors of production.

[4] Smith, *Wealth of Nations* II, p. 60.
[5] Gunnar Myrdal, *Asian Drama*, (New York: Twentieth Century Fund, 1968), pp. 442–50 and 506–10.
[6] Harry Williams, *Ceylon, Pearl of the East*, 5th ed., (London: Robert Hale Ltd., 1956), p. 191.

In some colonies (Australia, New Zealand and North America) the emphasis on natural resources was less predominant. Here the main emphasis was on widely disparate factor endowments between the mother country and the newly acquired or newly discovered territory. Just as in the more tropical colonies, factor movement was necessary if the resources were to be fully developed and just as in the more tropical nations, the ultimate pattern of trade between the mother country and the territory was preordained. While non-competitive goods could be exported to the mother country from the colony, the most important exports (by volume) were likely to be goods using a great deal of land and these would be competitive with domestic production in the mother country (particularly when the colonies had temperate climates and exported grains). In this case, labour had to migrate and to settle (rather than to plan on a temporary stay). The migration of labour from the (overcrowded) mother country to the sparsely populated colony was induced by differences in the marginal product of labour in the two areas. These marginal products were translated into real wages. The rate of migration of labour and the concomitant migration of capital were both likely to be sensitive to conditions in the home country.[7] But there was probably some minimum difference required to induce migration and the mechanism of relative factor prices would identify relative shortages and induce the appropriate flow. The pattern of colonial development was quite different because of the intention of the expatriates to settle and therefore the colony did not endure the leakage of funds on imports from the mother country to reproduce 'home' nor the leakage into a fund of savings for retirement. The savings were invested in real assets and the spread effects, consequently, much greater.

The need for migration to take place before the colony could be successfully exploited means that the traditional explanation of migration as a substitute for trade does not hold for colonial possessions of this kind.

---

[7] See the theory of colonial development of Mill cited in Williams, 'The Theory Reconsidered', op. cit.

COMMERCIAL POLICY

Before the twentieth century, colonialism featured an excessive degree of mercantilism. This was the means by which the maximum share of gains from intra-empire trade could be made to accrue to the mother country. These measures can be described, in general terms, as commercial policy. But this was a commercial policy of regulations rather than of discriminating tariffs and subsidies. Indeed, to the extent that preference arrangements existed, they tended to protect the rights of colonial territories to serve the metropolitan markets. But, since the beneficiaries of those rights were mainly nationals of the mother country, the indigenous people of the colonies derived little benefit.

There are two distinct patterns of commercial policy. In colonies such as the nations of South Asia where the goods exported to the mother country were virtually exclusively type 1*A* non-competitive goods, there was little reason to interfere too minutely with the pattern of trade. The proviso was, of course, that manufactures from the mother country should enjoy a priority in the colony's imports. In one important case, the manufactures of the mother country were given priority over a domestic import-competing industry when the Indian cotton textile industry was subjected to severe competition in order to provide a market for Lancashire cotton.[8]

The second type of colony is one in which the comparative advantage of the colony in international trade lay primarily in a substantially different proportionate factor endowment in addition to certain industry-specific natural resources. When colonisation of this type had taken place, the concern of the mother country was to protect its own industry from colonial competition in class 2 competitive goods. The classic example of such a relationship was that between Great Britain and her North American possessions. The classic means of commercial policy for such a relationship was direct regulation and in the British—American case, the regulation used was the act of navigation that controlled the means of transportation of the exports of the colonies as well as their destination.

One interesting fact about the act of navigation was the very

---

[8] Vincent A. Smith, *The Oxford History of India* (3rd ed.), (Oxford: Clarendon Press, 1958), pp. 706—7.

clear distinction it drew between the different types of good and, particularly, between type 1*A* and 1*B* non-competitive imports into Britain.[9] The act of navigation limited the exportation of some of the American colonies' goods to Britain and, in this way, gave the British a monopsonistic advantage. Such commodities were the so-called enumerated commodities. Other goods could be exported directly to other countries ('in British or plantation ships') and were termed non-enumerated commodities. Type 1*A* commodities (Smith lists molasses, coffee, cacao-nuts, tobacco, pimento, ginger, whale-fins, raw silk, cottonwool, beaver and other peltry of America, indigo, fustic and other dying woods) were enumerated. For any surplus of American exports over British needs, Britain enjoyed a middleman position as well as a lucrative carrying trade. Type 1*B* commodities — gap-fillers — were enumerated only when American exports would not endanger domestic production. But, such American exports based on comparative advantage exclusive of industry-specific resource components, as would, in Smith's words, 'have interfered too much with the produce of the industry of our own people', were non-enumerated commodities. By limiting the sale of these commodities to countries south of Cape Finisterre, the British reduced the probability that imports taken back in the ships that had brought the exports would be manufactures competitive with British exports.

CONCLUSION

An analysis of the economic relationship between a colonial power and a colony requires a more complex theory than orthodoxy provides. The multiplicity of factors of production, the concept of non-competitive goods and a theory of international economics that can countenance trade flows and factor migration as being complementary, are all necessary. Non-competitive goods (and, therefore, industry-specific and immobile factors of production) are vital to any economic theory of tropical colonial development. Non-competitive goods are less important for the type of colonial development that is represented by the exploitation of sparsely-populated lands in

---

[9] Smith, *The Wealth of Nations* II, pp. 78–81.

temperate climates. The migration of factors to these colonies represented a reallocation of factors of production that increased global economic efficiency. For both types of colonies, the pattern of trade was predetermined by the large disparity in factor endowments and factor prices which migration and trade would never completely eradicate.

8 International Factor Mobility

Somewhat paradoxically, a theory of international trade should offer a set of basic analytical tools that will constitute a frame of reference for the analysis of the international movement of factors of production as well as of commodities and services. The argument that underlies this contention is the analogue of that which ranked the Heckscher–Ohlin theory above the Ricardian doctrine: that a theory of international trade should examine the effects of trade not only upon commodity prices, output and consumption but should also relate the effects of trade back to factor markets and prices and to income distribution. But there is an additional consideration. Factor movements have taken place on a very large scale since World War II and, in the process, have importantly affected the factor endowments of trading nations. In this sense, the analysis of international trade in commodities cannot be examined except in conjunction with an understanding of the international movements of factors of production. It should be a theory of international resource allocation rather than a simple theory of international trade.

There was in the economic thinking of the classicists a clear realization that factors of production, while to some degree mobile between countries, were markedly less mobile inter-than intra-nationally. This disparity was exaggerated so as completely to exclude the international mobility of factors of production from the study of international trade. The admitted simplification served a useful purpose in that it allowed the analysis of the causes and the repercussions of international trade to go forward with much greater precision and clarity. Current orthodox theory inherited this assumption of the international immobility of factors and used it for the same purpose. The assumption is prerequisite to any exact statement that used given factor supplies as the fundamental, trade-creating distinction between nations. In its extreme form, in which factor price equalization was deemed to have been brought about,[1] there existed neither the need for nor incentive to factors of production to migrate internationally. *Per contra*, orthodox theory does recognise that perfect international factor mobility could, if trade were impeded in any way, completely eliminate the need for trade in commodities by changing the original resource endowments in the two countries so as to generate identical proportional factor mixes.[2] Factor movements are, then, recognized as a potential substitute for the movement of goods between nations.

The recognition of only the two polar cases means that the orthodox theory has never been able to interrelate the simultaneous flows of goods and of factors. This shortcoming probably derives in no small measure from the static and equilibrium cast of the theory. In addition, the theory has misrepresented the real world. While completely unimpeded trade in commodities could eliminate the need for any international migration of factors — but not through factor price equalization — factor movements cannot, in a world with immobile industry-specific factors of production, completely eliminate the need for exchanges of commodities. Even in a world of perfect factor mobility, non-competitive goods would need to be traded.

The world has seen massive movements of factors among nations. Voluntary migrations by people from all parts of Europe to North America and willing movements of people from developing nations (often ex-colonies) to more affluent nations have taken place at the same time that massive amounts of capital has flowed both among developed nations and from rich to poor nations. The movement of both capital and labour have been accompanied by transfers of human capital and technology. Probably the most straight-forward way to consider whether a nation is relatively well endowed with a factor is to see whether the nation is a net exporter or a net importer of the factor. Of the five factors of production, four are potentially mobile among nations. Physical and human capital, proprietary

---

[1] See, for example, Bhagwati, *Journal of Political Economy*, (September/October 1972), p. 1052.

[2] R. A. Mundell first demonstrated this extreme and somewhat paradoxical case in 'International Trade and Factor Mobility', *American Economic Review* XLVII, (June 1957), pp. 321–35.

knowledge and unskilled labour can all migrate. Unskilled labour is necessarily generic but internationally-mobile capital can be either generic or industry-specific. Migrating human capital and proprietary knowledge are predominantly industry-specific. The purpose of this short chapter is to apply the generalized theory to the phenomenon of the international movement of factors of production. The voluntary migration of human beings is considered first and used to provide a framework that may be extended to include the other factors.

Studies of labour migration have always been made in a relatively realistic setting in which observable differences in living standards have been recognized as existing virtually steadily through time in different nations.[3] In such a dis-equilibrium framework, analysts have attempted to identify 'push' and 'pull' forces. The former include all those things that tend to drive a person to leave home — the forces of frustration, despair and dissatisfaction that can abound in a country of emigration. 'Pull' forces, on the other hand, embody all of those desirable traits in the country of immigration.

Economic forces are important elements in both push and pull forces and a quite reasonable first approach to an empirical study of migration could be set up using only economic explanatory variables. In such a model it would be difficult to distinguish the push and pull forces in some instances since the variable would be a difference between, say, two wage rates. The model would, necessarily, be short-term in concept and could be consonant with the generalized theory. The end-of-period wage rates would be the main indicator of the difference in living standards that would motivate the migration. However, such a theory would be only a first step in the analysis. A transitory wage differential would not be a sufficient motivation for migration. The duration of the differential over a number of years would need to be estimated before the potential migrant could be induced to travel. Further, the migrant would need to have knowledge of the availability to him of the foreign wage. The wage differential would be sensitive to the flows of migration that it induced since the

---

[3] In a similar context, Martin Shubik, 'A Curmudgeon's Guide to Micro-economics', *Journal of Economic Literature* VIII, (June 1970), pp. 416–17, notes that any serious study of a market's competitiveness requires that elegant abstract microtheory be left behind.

relative factor endowments of the two countries would be altered. The potential narrowing effect on the wage differential of the induced flow of labour may be negated by external disturbances and different rates of capital formation and/or rates of population growth.

Even if relative factor prices serve as an indicator for many other advantages that accrue to a migrant, they will not be the unique cause or determinant of migration. The certainty of the perceived gain is an important influence upon the decision to migrate. The gain must be conceived of in terms of a lump sum of real income (the present value) that will be acquired over a finite number of years. This lump sum serves as a measure of the desirability of migration. Against it must be counted the costs. Part of the costs of migration is subjective but part of it, transportation, is defined in money terms and can be contrasted directly with the expected gain. The size of the transportation cost item will discourage migration in two ways: the greater the cost, the larger is the required benefit and the greater the cost, the less the reversibility of the decision.

There is a clear similarity here to the underlying causes of international trade in goods. A difference in price is the determinant of factor movements just as it is the determinant of trade. The similarity extends to the possibility of impediments to the movement of factors being imposed in much the same way as tariffs interfere with the movement of goods. It was S. B. Linder who, in *An Essay on Trade and Transformation*, evolved the very valuable concepts of trade-creating and trade-braking forces.[4] The potential volume of trade between two countries was determined by trade-creating forces and the proportion of the potential volume actually achieved was decided by the strength of the trade-braking forces. Equivalent concepts, mobility-creating and mobility-braking forces, can usefully be employed to explain the international movement of factors of production. At the end of any period, there will be a difference between the real rate of return paid to a factor of production in the two countries. These differences may be taken as indicative of differences in living standards, particularly when the factor is unskilled labour. The difference would be measured in terms of money incomes converted to some

[4] pp. 102–9.

common numeraire by the rate of exchange. This difference in the price of the factor constitutes the major mobility-creating force. Against this single force must be set the several mobility-braking forces. Migration takes place if the real income differential exceeds the monetary value of the mobility-braking forces by some threshold amount. The mobility-braking forces can comprise anything from transportation costs, lack of knowledge of opportunities, uncertainty as to the availability and permanence of the wage difference, to governmental impediments to entry or exit. It may well be that any flow of migration is determined in the short run more by variation in the composition and size of the mobility-braking forces and that, for unskilled labour at least, the mobility-creating force is always great enough. Thus, flows of migrants would tend not to respond to small changes in wage differentials except through the wage differential being correlated with the magnitude of mobility-braking forces. This may explain the historic importance of rates of unemployment in the country of immigration and the existence of an advance guard of migrants in the country of (or area of) immigration.

Such a simple model would not distinguish among types of labour. The migration of skilled technicians has become a notable feature of the post-World War II world. The movement threatened to starve poor countries of human capital. With the exception of students who visited rich countries to gain and education and stayed to enjoy the affluence, international movements of human capital normally involve industry-specific capital. The migration of people with professional qualifications, the so-called brain drain, requires a multi-factor theory of international economics since the income-differentials can and will vary among professions. Often human capital moves from a poor to a rich nation in response to a short-run impediment to the supply of that type of capital in the country of immigration. This is particularly relevant when the end product of the factor is a service which is not transportable internationally. This type of migration is equivalent to trade in type $1B$ goods.

The movement of human capital is likely to have quite different types of mobility-braking forces. Ignorance of opportunities in the country of immigration is less likely to impede the movement of professionals who will enjoy a greater awareness of the world market for their services. Language barriers and lack of acquaintance are also likely to be less important for human capital since, frequently, the professional training carries with it the language and the acquaintance. The finality of migration may also be less for a highly skilled person since he or she may well be better able to re-establish the original position in the country of emigration should expectations abroad not be fulfilled. Social and cultural factors may be more important for professionals than for unskilled labour. The profession may well carry less prestige or renown in the country of immigration than 'at home'.

Governmental barriers to migration constitute important mobility-braking forces. Nations are concerned with the impact of migrants upon the welfare of those remaining in the country of migration and with the welfare of voting citizens in the country of immigration. Unskilled labour may have insuperable barriers raised against them, often as a result of lobbying by the labour movement. Such lobbying would be comparable to lobbying for tariffs on the importation of labour-intensive goods. Barriers to the entry of human capital can vary quite strongly among the different professions. For some (non-tariff) barriers in the form of legal requirements for professional licensing will be absolute. For other professions, the barriers may be surmountable by the payment of a tax — such as a protracted internship in hospitals at relatively low rates of pay. Attempts by governments of emigration nations to impede the outflow of human capital can also be absolute or may be surmountable by the payment of an exit tax. Such a tax often has a basic rationality in that the state has subsidized the acquisition of human capital by the migrant.

For human capital, the flow of migration may be more sensitive to variations in the mobility-creating force than is the flow of unskilled labour. But empirical studies of human capital flows suffer from the problems of the changing mix of migrating skills and the simultaneous variations in income differentials and barriers to entry and exit.[5]

The same analytic framework can be applied to the international transfer of capital and proprietary knowledge. Movement of both of these factors requires that the rate-of-return differen-

---

[5] Migration within the same nation probably enjoys a smaller wage differential (though rural—urban migration may make a substantial mobility-creating force) but much better knowledge and easier reversibility.

tial exceed the mobility-braking forces. The great difference between the migration of these factors and the migration of human beings is the smaller risk involved. A human being risks life and limb in the process of migration – the transfer of knowledge or capital involves far less vital dimensions.

The international flow of capital resembles the flow of human capital. There exist good markets for such transactions and the differentials, if any, are quoted regularly for debt capital. It is the mobility-braking forces of risk and of legal barriers to capital movements that will impede movements of capital. Legal barriers may be absolute. Risk can often be converted into a cost and in this way the decision to transfer capital abroad or to leave it at home is fairly straightforward. Debt capital placed abroad confronts three types of risk: exchange-rate risk, economic risk and expropriation risk. The economic risk (or uncertainty) exists independently of the location of the capital and can therefore be disregarded or allowed for in the locational decision-making process. Efficient secondary debt markets reduce any such exposure. Exchange rate risk can be eliminated by (sequential) forward cover. Expropriation risk (which must include the risk of non-repatriation of earnings as well as capital) has no safeguard except the history of the nation in which the capital is located and the vulnerability of any policy of expropriation to a counterpolicy by other nations. If these costs, plus any transactions costs, are deemed to be less than the differential in the rate or return, the capital will flow. As with the flow of human capital, the flow itself will tend to eliminate the advantageous income differential but this is less important for debt capital since the rate of return is computed at the moment of transfer. This is a clear indication of the greater speed of adjustment of capital markets.

Direct investment resembles the transfer of debt capital except that the mobility-braking forces are much larger for direct investment than for portfolio investment. Rates of return are not known and are subject to uncertainty, and there exists a greater risk of expropriation and of local political agitation that can be costly. The time horizon of direct investment is virtually infinite and a quick reversal is not possible. These greater mobility-braking forces affecting direct investment will make the differential rate of return between foreign investment and the alternative use of the capital much greater.

Proprietary knowledge can also be transferred to a resident of a foreign country and a return earned. The return is paid in the form of a royalty. There are costs to be set against this income. First is the potential return to the knowledge from exports to the knowledge-receiving country from home factories or from the establishment there of a foreign subsidiary. A second element in the cost is the sheer money cost of negotiating the licensing agreement. A third element is the possibility that the knowledge will be used for purposes other than those specified in the agreement and the return from the knowledge currently enjoyed in third countries will be reduced.[6]

The role of the colonial relationship in promoting the international movement of factors of production was the reduction of risk and the better knowledge of profitable opportunities for international factor movements. But, this movement was usually factor migration from rich regions to poor regions. Colonialism did not ordinarily result in a reverse flow of unskilled labour into the rich country. However, the colonial regulations quite frequently did include a nominal freedom of movement within the empire and thereby provided unskilled labour in colonial territories the right to creep under barriers to immigration into the colonial power. Metropolitan France, the United Kingdom and the United States have all experienced large influxes of unskilled labour from areas with erstwhile colonial relationships. For unskilled labour, the colonial relationship also facilitated migration by removing much of any language barrier.

Except under the most unusual circumstances, movement of factors of production from one nation to another will bring about an inter-period movement of the offer curves of the two nations. The movement of factors will have altered the relative factor endowments and will therefore have changed the optimum trading posture in both countries — even in the short run. The fact that physical capital, human capital and proprietary knowledge are all like to industry-specific suggests that

[6] The question of the choice between licensing and using the knowledge in a foreign subsidiary can be more suitably analyzed in terms of direct investment in chapter 9.

the effect of factor mobility will change the shapes as well as the position of the offer curves. In ordinary times, the effects of factor mobility upon international trade patterns will be difficult to distinguish from ordinary growth effects because the movement of factors will be small relative to the stock of factors extant in the country of immigration. But, over time, the impact of factor migration upon the pattern of international trade will become more apparent since factor flows are cumulative and tend to alter relative factor prices over time (relative to what they would have been in the absence of international factor mobility). Some transfers of factors can have quite short-run and obvious effects upon the pattern of international trade. These would be industry-specific factors that created a new industry in the country of immigration. Such an industry might be either an export industry (probably when foreign factors were united with immobile domestic natural resources) or an import-competing industry when industry-specific factors transformed a type $1C$ good into a type 2 or type 3 good.

When factor flows are large relative to the domestic supply of factors, severe dislocations and problems of adjustment may be experienced in the country of immigration. Dislocations of this type might well justify the temporary imposition of barriers to factor movements in order that the economy may suffer smaller costs of adjustment.[7]

---

[7] The rationale for such barriers to migration is similar to that for senile industry protection — see chapter 10 below.

9 Direct Investment and Multi-national Enterprise

Colonial ties facilitated the combination of capital and technology from rich countries with the cheap labour and natural resources of the colonial territories by reducing to a minimum the political and physical risks involved. Colonialism ceased to be an important force after World War Two and movements of factors have to take place between separate and sovereign states — albeit states of different military and economic power. These movements of factors can take place between the erstwhile colonial power and independent dominions (the United Kingdom and Canada and Australia) or between an erstwhile mother country and a tropical ex-colony (France and the Ivory Coast) and between nations that have never had peacetime political connections (Japan and Thailand). These flows of investment must all be seen as international investment and must involve the risk of expropriation or nationalization.

Direct investment takes place when a resident of one nation acquires operating control over a productive unit in a foreign country. The flow can cause a new productive unit to be created, can acquire an ongoing firm through a takeover or can expand an existing facility.[1] Multi-national enterprise is a subset of direct investment acquisitions, and can generally be taken to refer to large corporations with productive units operating in many countries. The operations of these subsidiaries are integrated with each other and with the productive units in the parent country in order to rationalize production and to achieve high profits. Some foreign subsidiaries, the results of direct investment, are not parts of multi-national enterprise. The actual distinction between international corporations and multi-national enterprise is not clearly definable.[2] In this

---

[1] See my *The Economics of Business Investment Abroad*, (London: The Macmillan Company, 1972), p. 14.
[2] *Ibid.*, pp. 71–3.

chapter, the terms will be used interchangeably unless the degree of operational integration in many nations has especial relevance for the argument.

Professor John H. Dunning has observed that the orthodox theory of international trade provides no analytic basis for the existence of multi-national corporations.[3] Given the sheer magnitude of this type of enterprise in the modern world, this failure is a serious shortcoming of the orthodox theory. The omission is, of course, inevitable since the multi-national corporation has as its fundamental characteristic the international movement of factors of production. While the process necessarily involves direct investment, multi-national enterprise almost always involves the international movement of cooperating factors of production. But the ability to allow for this movement is not enough. The theory of migration delineated in chapter 8 could account for the presence in a host nation of foreign capital, foreign skilled labour and foreign proprietary knowledge all under the direction of indigenous entrepreneurial control. The capital would be portfolio investment attracted by the rate of return in excess of that available to investors in the source or investing nation. Skilled technicians can be lured abroad by high salaries and the promise of exceptional working conditions and fringe benefits. Proprietary knowledge can be acquired through licensing. Thus, all the ingredients for a local undertaking can be derived from foreign sources and combined in a nation without the instigation of multi-national enterprise. A theory of international economics that can provide a basis for factor migration is necessary but not sufficient to explain the phenomenon of multi-national enterprise. The missing link is the theory of the firm. An explanation of multi-national enterprise requires a combination of the two theories. The basic questions to be answered are: 'what motivates a firm to establish foreign subsidiaries instead of supplying foreign markets through some different form of endeavour such as exporting or licensing?' and 'why can the necessary groups of factors of production most easily and effectively be united in a foreign nation under the aegis of a large international corporation?'

There are two different kinds of motivations that will induce

[3] *Oxford Economic Papers*, (November 1973), pp. 289–336.

a corporation to invest in a foreign nation. The motivation is either aggressive or defensive — aggressive to expand the volume or rate of profits as well as the scope of operations and defensive to protect the existing profit rate or scope of operations against potential inroads from competitors. Three aggressive and three defensive motivations can usefully be considered:

Aggressive Motivations

1. To realize potential economies that are internal to the firm.
2. To exploit a knowledge advantage.
3. To establish presence in a foreign oligopoly and to share any oligopoly rents.

Defensive Motivations

1. To establish local production in a foreign market to preserve a market share obtained by exports.
2. To acquire a sure source of raw materials to serve the domestic production complex.
3. To acquire raw material deposits to preserve a barrier to entry into a global oligopoly.

The spread of operations that ensues from obeying any of these six motivations will involve either vertical or horizontal integration. The purpose of this chapter is to show how the generalized theory does provide the necessary international basis to serve in combination with a theory of the firm in order to provide an analytic base for the existence of multi-national enterprise. The theories of the firm will be drawn from the works of R. H. Coase and R. E. Caves. The concepts developed by Coase portray the economies that are internal to the firm mainly through vertical integration.[4] Caves' analysis has brought together the corporate gains that can be achieved by horizontal integration in different national, imperfectly competitive markets and the gains that can derive from the international

---

[4] See R. H. Coase, 'The Nature of the Firm', *Economica* n.s. IV (1937), 386–405, reprinted in *Readings in Price Theory*, G. J. Stigler and K. E. Boulding (eds.) (Homewood, Ill.: Richard D. Irwin, Inc., 1952) pp. 331–51.

transfer of proprietary knowledge as a source of quasi-rents to be earned by foreign subsidiaries.[5]

Economies of internal organization necessarily are available only to corporations which have operations covering more than one production process under their control. These economies derive from the substitution of internal organization for 'the cost of using the price mechanism'[6] The costs of using the price mechanism are the costs of search, the costs of negotiation and contract, lack of precise control over the timing of shipments and similar phenomena. These areas offer potential gains from the coordination of activities within a single organization to reduce the costs of inputs, to reduce the uncertainties of scheduling and related costs and, from a sense of control over the various stages of production, to enable a corporation to plan an undertaking on a large scale that requires for its success, a compatibility of equipment and method throughout.

The secret of obtaining potential Coase-economies is coordination of different stages of treatment and such coordination can most easily be achieved by common executive control. This process is generally referred to as vertical integration and can involve investments that point forward to the consumer as well as backward to the primary materials.

Vertical integration is, except for the inherent costs of doing business in a foreign country, indifferent to national boundaries. The usual way for vertical integration to involve international investment is through the acquisition of a source of basic raw materials. To the extent that the raw material is an industry-specific, internationally immobile factor of production and therefore a potential non-competitive good, international investment is mandatory if the corporation is to acquire direct control over a source of the basic raw materials. Another common form of vertical integration that involves foreign investment is the creation of a sales subsidiary in a foreign market supplied with exports from the parent company. This type of subsidiary will be created only by firms that market a differentiated good and its existence is based upon the belief that a foreign sales subsidiary is more efficient than a foreign

[5] Caves, 'International Corporations: The Industrial Economics of Foreign Investment', *Economica* n.s. (February 1971), pp. 1—27.
[6] Coase, *Economica* n.s. IV, p. 390.

sales agent so that the foreign subsidiary offers a Coase-economy in marketing.

Backward integration to acquire raw material sources could be avoided by normal dealings in the raw material market and/or by long-term contracts with producing companies.[7] While the acquisition of raw material sources does offer the possibility of an economic rent, it is the ongoing economies of vertical integration which are the more important consideration in the decision to invest abroad. In addition to the benefits which derive from vertical integration independent of its international dimensions, international vertical integration offers a corporation a degree of flexibility which can be used to good advantage. Usually the main reason for the creation of a foreign subsidiary involving vertical integration is the existence of an activity which is not mobile internationally. The next activity and the ensuing activities in the productive sequence can be 'footloose'. The international corporation obtains in this way the possibility of additional Coase-economies if the relative national cost structures allow additional operations to be performed with profit in the foreign country.

The initiative to invest abroad in order to develop an internationally immobile resource may derive from a particular kind of knowledge that affords the entrepreneur in the developed or investing country an advantage over his counterpart in the resource-owning nation. Knowledge of the market for a particular primary product in the developed nation may lead to its development by direct investment abroad. Ultimately, this knowledge may lead to the establishment of a combined operation involving Coase-economies but in the first instance, the development of the product may be done simply to serve the anticipated market.

This ability to coordinate activities internationally and to locate footloose activities in that country of operation in which marginal costs are the least, is the primary contribution to global economic efficiency of the multi-national corporation. The greater the number of nations in which the multi-national enterprise has subsidiaries located, the larger is the number of potential opportunities to take advantage of variations in

[7] Ibid., pp. 391–2.

international costs and, what may not be the same thing, comparative advantage.

A nation's price competiveness in any particular activity does not pre-require the existence of a local subsidiary but the benefits of internal coordination may be sufficiently great to warrant the establishment of a subsidiary simply for the purpose of combining a small foreign cost advantage with the potential Coase-economies. This kind of foreign manufacturing operation might result in the creation of a parts-manufacturing concern in a foreign nation. It may be that the parent corporation cannot find an indigenous firm with the requisite knowhow in the country in which costs are the lowest. A second reason for preferring a subsidiary to a contract purchase is the ability of the parent to set quality control and inspection standards in the wholly owned subsidiary and to integrate these with domestic quality control procedures. Such an investment might be induced by an increase in the ability of a developing country to produce manufactured goods (a change in the proportionate endowment of human capital and/or a change in the modifier of the production function), by a change in the relative cost structure between the importing and the host country or by a change in the cost structure within the firm. Such a change in the firm's internal cost structure could result from a labour contract that makes foreign manufacture of some operations feasible.[8]

Direct foreign investment in an enclave industry has the distinct advantage that it enables the multi-national corporation to achieve the benefits of the national resource endowment in the host nation without the concomitant cost of the effects of the national modifier to production functions. The avoidance of the modifier will be one reason for indigenous workers in the enclave industry to have higher marginal products and, therefore, higher wages.

The other way in which Coase-economies can be achieved is through financial integration of operations in various enterprises. If different parts of a commercial enterprise generate surplus cash flows and deficit cash needs at different times, the available funds can be used to economize on working capital can be used for investments in different subsidiaries according

---

[8] See below in this chapter, pp. 156–7.

to the overall needs of the enterprise. Sheer size of operations does provide the parent firm and its subsidiaries with potential advantages in credit markets as well and a foreign subsidiary may, through its parent, enjoy access to a foreign low-cost capital market that would not be available to it as an independent entity.

Foreign investment in an extractive industry may also follow from a need on the part of a large corporation to acquire a sure source of raw materials for its domestic production operations — a defensive motivation. Acquisition of such resources through foreign investment has enabled large firms to conserve their own domestic raw materials, if any, as well as to develop low cost sources. This type of investment can be viewed as a special type of internal economy but it may also have as its cause the desire of executives to rest better at night.

Of the four remaining motivations for foreign investment, the profitable utilization of an asset is the basis for two and market imperfections in a more traditional sense of oligopolistic structure are the basis for the other two. But, it is not possible always to draw a hard and fast line of distinction among the two sets of causation. For example, the exploitation of a piece of proprietary knowledge may be a sufficient reason for establishing a foreign manufacturing subsidiary but if the knowledge is most likely to be found in differentiated goods industries and these industries have oligopolistic market structures then it may be difficult to assess primary responsibility. It is also possible that the proprietary knowledge may be necessary before the decision is made to attempt to insert a subsidiary into a foreign oligopoly. Either exploitation in a foreign country of an asset or entry into a foreign oligopolistic market requires the duplication of a particular activity in a second country rather than the addition of a complementary activity. These motivations involve horizontal integration rather than vertical integration — Caves-economies rather than Coase-economies underlie the following paragraphs. In an international frame of reference, horizontal integration can be defined as producing abroad (usually for sale abroad) commodities which are the same as, or generically similar to, those produced by the parent company domestically. Horizontal expansion takes place when a foreign subsidiary is, actually or potentially, a source of competition with the domestic production of a similar commodity. Almost necessarily this process hinges upon some manufacturing activity.

The fundamental reason for the creation of a manufacturing subsidiary in a foreign market is that foreign manufacture will enable the parent company to derive a return from an asset that exceeds the return available through other means. This asset must be privately held and unique to the investing corporation, internationally mobile and applicable in foreign nations at a return that exceeds any marginal costs of transfer by a significant margin.[9] The most common asset of this type is some element of knowledge which is either unknown to competitors or protected from imitation and which offers to the manufacturing process either a reduction in costs or a sales advantage. Knowledge can take the form of design experience, specific marketing knowhow or productive technology. In essence, the piece of proprietary knowledge offers a competitive advantage to the holder which can be transformed into additional profit through its utilization in a new geographical location.

Indigenous entrepreneurs in a nation ordinarily enjoy a cost advantage in competing with foreigners due to their familiarity with local customs, their knowledge of the local markets and, possibly, as a result of (covert) preferential treatment by the domestic government. The decision to invest in a foreign country depends upon the price of exports from the parent company relative to the price of competing goods sold by indigenous firms and on the possibility of more efficiently meeting the competition of domestic firms by establishing a foreign subsidiary which will replace the exports. The difference between the landed cost of exports (imports) and local, foreign production depends upon four things: comparative advantage, the advantage to indigenous firms, the advantage derived from any proprietary knowledge utilized in the exporting factors and on the costs of impediments to international trade such as tariffs and transportation costs.[10] The significant feature of proprietary knowledge is that it can be moved geographically at

---

[9] Motivation 4 — to preserve a market share — involves the preservation of the positive return to an existing asset in place of its destruction by foreign competition. The causation is quite similar, see below pp. 153—4.

[10] This argument is developed in detail in *The Economics of Business Investment Abroad*, pp. 81—91.

a relatively small cost and combined with other factors of production in the most profitable location. Therefore, if a nation has a comparative advantage in the production of a commodity with reference to its endowments of physical and human capital, natural resources and labour, that advantage may be enhanced or eliminated by proprietary knowledge. If comparative advantage is enhanced by the proprietary knowledge, the foreign market will be supplied by exports. If the advantage is not enough to overcome barriers to international trade, the market will be supplied domestically and the good will be a non-tradeable good. If, under these circumstances, the proprietary knowledge outweighs the cost advantage of indigenous firms, foreign investment will take place.[11] Clearly, what is specified here is the existence of a sufficient mobility-creating force and the argument does not consider here its possible frustration by mobility-braking forces.

Product differentiation may reinforce the gains from proprietary knowledge or may be prerequisite to its existence. There are three ways by which product differentiation can give rise to, knowledge that will be likely to make a foreign subsidiary a feasible concept. Differentiated goods have design features and performance-specifications that distinguish them from their competitors. These features allow individual tastes to supplement price in buyers' choices. The fact that these design distinctions are an integral part of the product means that the design features actually retained will have proven desirability and will have been protected by patent. Long experience in the production of the commodity will have provided the manufacturer with specialist knowhow in production or special cost-reducing production processes. Finally, the experience in the home market will have provided the international corporation with a competitive advantage in marketing and sales strategy.

The sheer size of the international corporation might provide it with a cost-advantage sufficient to overcome any advantages accruing to relatively small domestic manufacturers. It is improbable that a firm would institute a foreign subsidiary while economies of scale in production or marketing still exist in its domestic operations. Any such gains would be likely to

[11] The role of tariffs is taken up below.

exceed the expected profits to be derived from foreign manufacture. Once domestic capacity is fully utilized, then foreign investment may take place in the course of the so-called product cycle but any such investment owes its existence to the general preferability of foreign manufacture rather than to the size of the international firm *per se*.

The rate of effective protection afforded to domestic producers of competing goods will constitute an important reason for manufacturing abroad as can the sheer costs of transporting exports. The difference between the landed cost of imports and the costs of local manufacture can be crucial in any decision to create manufacturing capacity abroad. The elimination of the possibility of supplying the foreign market by exporting is virtually prerequisite to foreign direct investment. Once export supply has been eliminated, the choice is reduced to neglect of the market, licensing or foreign investment and, licensing excepted, to the relative cost advantages offered by local familiarity and proprietary knowledge. Differentiated goods are likely to be fairly sensitive to tariff protection because of quite high marginal rates of substitution between domestic and imported goods. Foreign investment is quite likely to involve differentiated goods sold by large corporations in relatively imperfectly competitive national markets.[1,2]

Licensing is an alternative to foreign investment. If exports are effectively blockaded and the mobility-braking forces exceed expected profit rates, then licensing may prove to be the only means by which a firm can earn a quasi-rent from its acquired knowhow. Reasons for choosing foreign investment in preference to licensing as a means of exploiting a piece of knowledge are the difficulties in the negotiation of the original royalty agreement and the difficulties of incorporating into such an agreement any new, second-generation pieces of knowledge that might be generated by the research and development facilities of the licensor. Licensing will tend to be less frequently used when the proprietary knowledge is expected to be a flow rather than a single isolated piece. However, if mobility-braking forces are small, even a one-shot piece may

[1,2] See Caves, *Economica*, Feb. 1971, *passim* for impressive evidence supporting this view. Note that because proprietary knowledge is industry-specific, direct international investment can take place in opposite directions simultaneously.

be useful in the foreign investment process. The per-unit cost saving derived from such a piece of knowledge might well make feasible the penetration of a tightly-knit foreign oligopolistic market. The cost advantage would provide the impetus that enables the firm to overcome the barriers to entry and to earn for itself membership in the oligopoly and a share in the quasi-rents that such membership affords. In the same way, the advantages to indigenous manufacturers might be expected to attentuate over time and the one-shot piece of proprietary knowledge might enable a firm to offset this disadvantage. One-shot pieces of knowledge are likely to have their value (measured in terms of the cost advantage that they provide) reduced over time as foreign competitors gain partial or complete access to the knowledge.

It is possible for a manufacturing subsidiary to be established in order to defend the asset already acquired in the form of an ongoing sales organization in a foreign market. Such a sales organization that sold goods shipped from the domestic factories, might suddenly find its source of supply rendered uncompetitive by a tariff or by the local establishment of another foreign subsidiary equipped with knowhow equal to that of the parent corporation. Under such circumstances, the international corporation would be faced with the alternatives of supplying the sales force from a factory within the host nation or of allowing its sales and marketing organization to wither away. Possession of an established market share and the sales organization that accompanies such possession, provides a firm with a competitive advantage for its products in the future. An ongoing sales organization represents a barrier to entry for would-be entrants into the market and, as such, is capable of earning a quasi-rent. The value of this asset can be computed by calculating the present value of these quasi-rents. Call the asset that these quasi-rents represent 'goodwill'. It becomes acceptable to create a foreign manufacturing subsidiary that would not be intra-marginal solely on its own account, when the present value of the difference between the required rate of profit and the expected rate of profit is less than the present value of the 'goodwill' of the sales organization. Such a strategy implies that the alternative policy of allowing the sales organization and the market share to contract temporarily and to expand again at a later date is a more costly strategy than supplementing the sales organization with a local production unit.

Sharing oligopoly rents would clearly constitute a motive for investing abroad to any firm provided that the present value of the rents would exceed the (current) costs of effecting entry into a tightly knit foreign market. Oligopolistic markets are likely to exist in differentiated goods in which existing sales organizations, brand names and distribution networks earn quasi-rents for the members of the oligopoly and permit them to maintain the oligopolistic market. To enter such a market a firm will require great financial resources since the entrant must be able to launch the necessary advertising campaign, to finance the establishment of sales and distribution organizations and, possibly, to fend off the destructive pricing policies that the existing oligopolists will inflict upon the entrant. If the oligopoly rents are sufficiently high, the prospect of a share in these rents will prove attractive enough to warrant the costs of entry. If the oligopolists have influence over the level of any tariff protection through political influence and are able effectively to blockade sales from foreign-based production units, then the rents can be that much greater and the attraction to achieve a share of them also that much greater.

This process by which entrants are attracted into high-yielding markets, will tend to equalize profit rates in an industry in all countries in which direct foreign investment is possible. If oligopolists ignore the transitory costs of barriers to entry, they will invest wherever in the world the return is highest and the forces of competition within the industry will tend to equalize returns in all nations. This would not eliminate the excess profits provided that there is some barrier to entry into the global industry. Once the decision to enter into a market has been made, the entrant will use in the host country any proprietary knowledge that it possesses. Further, the interaction of global oligopolists in different nations will presumably be beneficial to the host nations, at least in the short run, as the entry into the market must bias the outcome toward a lowering of oligopoly rents.

The process of foreign investment involving vertical integration — particularly backwards integration — may also be due to oligopolistic market structure. Caves suggests that the reduction of uncertainty and the desire to assure a future source of supply of a raw material may be supplemented as a motivation for investment by the hope that establishing a firm claim to a raw material source will help to preserve the existing global oligopoly. The foreign investment would deny potential entrants access to a necessary input. Such a possibility has serious implications for host countries that are poor and that must rely to a large extent upon the exportation of mineral deposits.

The international movement of factors of production under the auspices of a multi-national enterprise can be explained only when a theory of the firm is integrated with a theory of international resource allocation. The potential availability of Coase- and Caves-economies make direct investment profitable despite the exposure of owned assets to interference by host governments and by host-country politicos. But there is another important aspect of the transfer of factors of production internationally that makes the spread of the multi-national corporation even more likely to be the instigator of such mobility.

The potential gain from direct international investment may be keyed to the creation of a particular activity or to the transfer of a particular owned asset. Either of these measures on which an intra-marginal rate of return is to be achieved may well require that a group of complementary factors of production be moved to the foreign country. These factors of production will be industry-specific and may be unobtainable in the host country from indigenous sources. It may not be impossible for an individual entrepreneur, perhaps one indigenous to the host country, to assemble the necessary combination of factors of production but it is much more probable that an international enterprise will be able to do so and to do so more cheaply or more profitably than an individual entrepreneur could expect to. If the key factor is a piece of proprietary knowledge, there may be a need to utilize this knowledge in a production process with industry-specific cooperating factors of production. The firm that possesses the proprietary knowledge will have knowledge of and access to the cooperating factors.[13] It is likely to have such factors of production available within

---

[13] Knowledge in the case of a horizontally integrated subsidiary might involve familiarity with a particular set of machines that can be sold to the subsidiary.

its own network of operations. Such factors could be transferred more easily by an international corporation. This is
particularly true of human capital. Skilled technicians and
professionals may not be willing to move internationally to
work for an individual entrepreneur because of the interruption
that such an arrangement might bring about in the achievement
of their career goals. An international corporation can assure its
professional employees that service with a foreign subsidiary
will not only not interrupt their professional advancement but
might well enhance such advancement. Similarly, the international corporation can assure its employees of the continuation
of retirement benefits. Some pieces of knowledge are not
susceptible to licensing and may involve commercial secrets that
can only be entrusted to employees whose fidelity can be relied
upon. Finally, an international corporation by virtue of the
economies that it expects to achieve can probably be more
generous in its remuneration of humans than an individual
entrepreneur and may well perceive a larger profit from the
foreign investment simply because of the economies it will
achieve in mobilizing the needed combination of resources. The
argument is much the same for an investment involving a
vertical integration — particularly with the establishment of a
sales organization in a foreign country.

One aspect of the use of vertical integration by multi-national
corporations is the possibility that the transfer of assets to
foreign nations may be designed to supplant the same activity
in the home country. The possibility that a corporation might set
up a foreign manufacturing subsidiary to supply the home
market through its existing sales organization is a special case of
the ability of a multi-national enterprise to exploit potential
differences in the money costs of production in different
countries. The normal concept of foreign investment is for
foreign factories to serve foreign markets and for the parent
organization to import from its subsidiaries only when the
subsidiary produces non-competitive goods. It is possible for the
manufacturing capacity in the home country to cease to be
competitive with foreign subsidiaries and for a foreign subsidiary to replace the home productive capacity as the source of
supply for the existing and highly developed domestic sales and
marketing organization. The possibility of this type of investment can severely limit the bargaining ability of a labour union.

The Coase-economies make employees in a high-wage subsidiary of a multi-national corporation more vulnerable to layoff than employees in a similar but national endeavour. The decision to 'move abroad' can come with devastating swiftness and, in addition to decimating the membership of an industrial union, can leave large amounts of industry-specific and non-transferable human capital valueless.[14] The more footloose the activity, the smaller is the bargaining power of factors engaged in that activity. Technological innovation can also bring about an increase in the ability of a firm to transfer an operation to a foreign subsidiary — make an activity more footloose — when new machinery is developed that can substitute precision in the machine for precision needed by the operative. This techno-logical change would reduce the need for human capital and make the operation more easily transferable to country in which the ratio of unskilled labour to human capital was greater. Tariffs, and particularly tariffs with high effective rates of protection, can seriously reduce the ability of a firm to transfer an activity to a foreign source. In this sense, tariffs will protect workers and human capital engaged in potentially footloose activities.

Foreign direct investment will almost inevitably entail industry-specific disturbances for an ongoing pattern of trade. The creation of a foreign subsidiary may create imports into the investing country of non-competitive imports, of intermediate goods and possibly of finished goods. Equally, a foreign subsidiary can replace exports of finished products and increase exports of intermediate goods. Foreign investment will affect both the shape and the position of an offer curve. This, in turn, will affect the value of r^* and, through that, can alter the profitability of other tradeable-goods industries. By altering the pattern of trade, the establishment of a subsidiary will alter the intensity of demand for different factors of production and income distribution in the investing nation.

Any shift in an offer curve (or a change in shape) is likely to be relatively small between any two successive periods. Direct foreign investment flows are small relative to the volume of domestic capital formation and to the stock of capital and knowhow in the countries directly concerned. There is probably

[14] See *The Economics of Business Investment Abroad*, pp. 198–213.

a tendency for the effects of direct investment to be proportionately less important the larger are the countries and the industries concerned. For a small country, a large investment in an important industry could have important effects upon the pattern of trade even in a short period. But the effects of foreign direct investment are likely to be cumulative as the direction of flow of transfer of resources between nations is likely to be the same for many years. The cumulative effect can be very important. In addition to the more obvious effects of foreign investment on the pattern of trade of products of an individual industry, Lawrence B. Krause has suggested that the receipt of steadily increasing flows of dividends and interest could eliminate competitive goods (type 2 goods) from the list of manufactured exports of the United States.[15]

The establishment of multi-national corporations in the full sense of the expression leads to quite rapid transfers of knowledge and reduces the time taken between the application of the proprietary knowledge item at home and its transfers to foreign economies. Confidence of business executives that they could successfully integrate foreign subsidiaries and domestic capacity into a more profitable form of enterprise coincided roughly with the formation of the European Economic Community. Together, these two forces constituted two important increases in mobility-creating forces and led to a surge of direct investments out of the United States in the late 'fifties and early 'sixties. This increase in the range and scope of direct foreign investment brought about a permanent change in the length of time which American manufacturing industries served foreign markets with type $1C$ imports from a particular piece of knowledge and therefore permanently reduced the flow of that type of export to the detriment of the r^* of the United States.

To include direct international investment and multi-national business into the theory of international trade and resource reallocation has required each of the dimensions that the generalized theory has forced on to its orthodox base. The short-run framework is necessary if international factor movements are to be consistent with the theory. Investments that derive from Coase-economies need the concepts of inter-

---

[15] 'Trade Policy for the Seventies', *Columbia Journal of World Business*, (January/February, 1971) pp. 5–14.

nationally immobile factors of production (R)[16] and non-competitive imports. Those that derive from Caves-economies require the existence within the theory of proprietary knowledge and differentiated goods. Both types of investments must allow for scalars and modifiers to emphasize the effective differences between the production functions in the investing and host nations.

---

[16] In this context, natural resources must include the existence of a sales organization in the investing and importing nation because of the international immobility of the resource.

10 Commercial Policy

The orthodox theory of international trade has not provided a very fertile ground for the examination of the effects of commercial policy measures upon the composition of international trade flows.[1] The theory's emphasis on two-good models meant that variation in tariff structure could not be effectively analysed and the complete reliance upon generic factors of production excluded the concept of tariffs generating potentially permanent or short-run quasi-rents to industry-specific factors of production. Orthodoxy has sought to combine tariffs with its own artificial assumptions rather than to evolve to provide a frame of reference in which questions of commercial-policy effects can be fruitfully analysed. Orthodox theory has two main tenets for the implications of tariffs and non-tariff barriers (NTBs). A commercial policy measure will lead to the substitution of domestically produced goods for competing imports (if foreign supply is perfectly price-inelastic, a quota must be used) and, through this substitution, will bring about an 'inward' shift in the offer curve of the nation imposing the commercial policy measure. In this way, the country's net barter terms of trade will be improved as long as the trading partner's offer curve is not perfectly elastic. The question of the optimum tariff is one aspect of this branch of analysis. The second tenet relates commercial policy to income distribution and relies mainly on the classic Stolper—Samuelson article.[2] This article and the writing that it provoked[3] showed that the real income of the scarce factor will be enhanced by commercial

[1] The application of orthodox theory to the problem of smugglin (commercial policy evasion) proved to be extremely confining almost to the point of sterility. See Jagdish Bhagwati and Bent Hansen, 'A Theoretical Analysis of Smuggling', *Quarterly Journal of Economics* (May 1973), pp. 172—87 and Gray and Ingo Walter, 'Smuggling and Economic Welfare: A comment', *Quarterly Journal of Economics*, (November 1975), pp. 643—50.

[2] Wolfgang F. Stolper and Paul A. Samuelson, 'Protection and Real Wages', in Ellis and Metzler (eds.), *Readings in the Theory of International Trade*, (Homewood, Ill.: Irwin, 1966), pp. 333—57.

[3] Caves, *Trade and Economic Structure*, pp. 69—72.

policy. Add to that gain in real income the result of any favourable movement of the terms of trade and the argument is strengthened.

The additional variables that distinguish the generalized theory from orthodoxy do allow a significantly greater range of real-world problems to be analysed. Scale economies are vital to analysis of the infant-industry argument, multiple goods must be included in the frame of reference if effective rate of protection is to be contrasted with nominal rates, the short-period framework does permit short-run gains from commercial policy to be taken into account, and industry-specific factors of production enhance analysis of the income-distributional effects of a tariff. The generalized theory's contribution to analyses of commercial policy can be considered in three sections: (*a*) the broader range of the multi-good framework; (*b*) income-distributional implications; and (*c*) dynamic arguments for protection.[4]

The multi-good framework and the existence of industry-specific factors of production lay the groundwork for a consideration that the probability that a tariff will be imposed will vary with the degree of competitiveness of the import with domestic production. Graham was probably correct when he argued that the likelihood of a tariff being imposed was directly correlated with the sensitivity of the demand for imports to a tariff.[5] In Graham's two-country multi-commodity model in which all goods could be made in both countries, Graham argued that the cost of protection to the focus nation would be smaller if tariffs were employed to reduce imports of those goods just below the dividing line as the cost of domestic replacement would be less and 'the result is to secure those goods as imports which would cost a great deal more to produce at home than to import, and to secure them with exports which cost less per unit of important than before the protection'.[6] The introduction of differentiated goods must weaken that logic slightly since, in the generalized theory, differentiated goods are located at or near the top and bottom of the ranking. However,

---

[4] 'Tariffs' is used as a general expression for commercial policy unless a specific NTB is required for the argument.

[5] *Readings in the Theory of International Trade*, pp. 311–12, especially footnote 20.

[6] *Ibid.*, footnote 20.

the substitutability of domestic differentiated goods for imported ones is likely to be quite high and the loss in gain from trade from tariffs on differentiated goods negligible. There is, of course one *caveat* that must be added to the inference that trade in differentiated goods produces only a small gain from trade: this is probably true in the customary way of conceiving of gains from trade but the gain from trade in differentiated goods may derive from the effect foreign competition has on the efficiency of the domestic differentiated-goods industries.[7]

If Graham's thinking is correct, it would seem reasonable to expect a complete absence of tariffs on imports of non-competitive goods. Orthodox theory's assumption that both or all goods can be produced in both countries does not allow for this type of analysis. Excepting goods which are socially undesirable and are therefore subject to a zero quota as well as to legal penalty, tariffs on type 1*A* or 1*C* non-competitive goods serve only to reduce imports and foreign exchange expenditures without providing any direct benefit to an import-competing domestic industry. With type 1*B* goods, the results are different. Type 1*B* goods are produced domestically but supply is perfectly price-inelastic (see figure 3-1). A tariff will raise the price to the domestic consumer and will, therefore, allow the domestic industry to charge higher prices and to enhance its own profitability. More precisely, it is the scarce industry-specific factor of production that will reap the gain as a quasi-rent attributable directly to the protection. Imperfections in factor markets may permit cooperating factors of production to share the quasi-rents with the scarce industry-specific factor. For types 1*A* and 1*C* goods there is no difference between a tariff and an excise tax of the same *ad valorem* rate. For type 1*B* goods, a tariff provides a quasi-rent to the domestic industry while an excise tax on the type 1*B* good serves to raise government revenues and to reduce imports without providing any benefits to the domestic industry. Clearly for any type 1 good an excise tax is a good revenue source since it reduces consumption without affecting the prosperity of a domestic industry and, when the demand for the import is price-inelastic, it is possible to shift a significant amount of the burden of the tax on to the foreign supplier.[8]

[7] Differentiated goods are considered in detail in chapter 11.
[8] See Harry G. Johnson, *Economic Policies Toward Less Developed Countries*, (Washington: The Brookings Institution, 1967), p. 88.

Effective rates of protection analyses are concerned with the implications of tariff structure for the degree of protection afforded by different rates of nominal tariffs on goods at different stages of the productive process.[9] Such analyses can only be carried out in a multi-good framework in which intermediate goods and primary products can be traded contemporaneously with finished goods. The analysis must concern value added in different stages of the production process and can explain the establishment of so-called 'twin plants' on either side of the Mexican—US border so that different activities can be accomplished in different countries. Such was the influence of the orthodox theory that this whole extremely important aspect of the impact of commercial policy was first broached only in 1955.[10] The existence of effective rates of protection that differ widely from the nominal rate can create quite spectacular rates of effective protection for different activities with all the opportunity for quasi-rents for favoured groups that such protection allows. In addition, effective protection of activities at high rates can both severely affect the global allocation of scarce resources and possibly shift the burden of the tax on to primary producing countries that are either less developed or developing and which can ill afford it.[11] There is no satisfactory explanation of the way in which developed nations grasped the principle and advantages of a cascading tariff structure whereby higher rates are charged on goods as they approach the final stage. One possible explanation is that when the process of industrialization first took hold, the manufacturing nations had adequate domestic natural resources and processing industries grew with the industry. As these natural resources were exhausted and foreign sources located, there was an argument in favour of the preservation of the domestic processing industry. Quite a low nominal tariff rate was found to provide all that was needed to preserve the viability of the domestic processing industry. Unfortunately,

[9] For an excellent survey article see Herbert G. Grubel, 'Effective Tariff Protection: A Non-specialist Introduction to Theory, Policy, Implications and Controversies', in Grubel and Harry G. Johnson (eds.), *Effective Tariff Protection*, (Geneva: General Agreement of Tariffs and Trade and Graduate Institute of International Studies, 1971), pp. 1—15.

[10] In Clarence L. Barber, 'Canadian Tariff Policy', *Canadian Journal of Economics and Political Science*, XXI, (November 1955), pp. 513—30.

[11] See Johnson, *Economic Policies Toward Less Developed Countries*, pp. 90—104.

although the processing industry might well have been, properly, a senile industry[12] it managed to preserve itself through protection. The further stage of cascading that involved a still higher nominal rate on finished goods, may have come into being merely to ensure some higher rate of protection of that activity or simply by a misplaced belief that the same rate of nominal protection would have yielded zero protection to the final stage of processing.

Type 1*B* goods also raise interesting examples of commercial policy practices. The reason is that protection of agricultural goods has long been considered necessary in nations in which agriculture is a type 1*B* good. The main purpose of this type of commercial policy is to preserve the level of income of the farmer and great ingenuity has been applied to that end. The straightforward quota is the usual means of protecting agriculture because of the small elasticity of foreign supply of agricultural products. Both 'variable levies' and 'import calendars' are devices designed to protect non-competitive goods. Variable levies consist of import surcharges (sometimes combined with quotas) imposed to maintain the domestic price within a range deemed acceptable. Thus, if the world harvest is a good one, the levy might be quite high but, *per contra*, if world prices are high, then the import surcharge might be quite small. Import calendars usually protect crops that are potentially competitive with foreign goods only for a defined period of the year — thus, during the period of domestic production or harvesting of a crop, imports would be banned. When the domestic harvest is over, imports would be freely permitted. This type of arrangement recognizes that an agricultural good can change from type 1*A* to type 2 during the course of the year.[13]

The income-distributional effect of a tariff must derive from the advantages to import-substitutes industries and the factors that they employ, of increases in their output and from the concomitant decreases in output in export industries — assuming balanced trade and full employment are to prevail.

If perfect domestic product and factor markets exist, the effect of a tariff will be felt through its impact upon the output

---

[12] See below in this chapter.

[13] See Ingo Walter, 'Non-tariff Barriers and the Free-trade Area Option', Banca Nazionale del Lavoro *Quarterly Review*, (March 1969), p. 21–2.

mix and, through that, on the changed demand for factors of production. This, of course, is true almost by definition in long-run equilibrium and is the logic underlying the Stolper–Samuelson argument. Stolper–Samuelson also show that this result is, in perfect factor markets, independent of the consumption mix of either factor. The two-factor model excludes possible perverse factor mixes and therefore reduces the question of the impact of tariffs on income distribution to its simplest elements. The generalized theory adds three dimensions to the interrelationship between commercial policy and income distribution: the multiplicity of goods, the multiplicity of factors of production (including the existence of industry-specific factors), and the short-period frame of reference.

When trade takes place in many goods simultaneously, the imposition of a tariff on one import will rearrange the production and consumption mix in both countries. Demand for the protected import-substitute will increase and, in the absence of retaliation, some exports will experience declining demand as r^* changes. In the trading-partner nation, similar rearrangements of the production mix will take place. However, it is quite possible that the tariff will be retaliated against and an export will be reduced by about the same quantum that the import-substitute managed to increase its output. Thus, the rearrangement of the output-mix may vary according to the means by which balanced trade (or current account) is restored. Further, the existence of goods with perverse mixes of generic factors of production suggests that the effect of a tariff on income distribution is potentially less straightforward than Stolper–Samuelson would imply. If the (import-substitute) good on which the tariff is levied has a perverse factor mix, then the imposition of a tariff may not increase the net demand for what is perceived to be the relatively scarce generic factor. If the export good, the output of which is reduced, also has a perverse factor mix then the net demand for the (perceived) relatively scarce factor will also be reduced. The (perceived) relatively scarce generic factor would not benefit from the imposition of a tariff under these conditions. To the extent that the tariff is imposed upon a good whose import-substitute is near the dividing line (in accordance with Graham's suggestion) and the good utilizes some industry-specific factor of production, the probability of a perverse factor-mix is relatively great. If the tariff is met by a retaliatory tariff on a single good that is itself not very far from the dividing line, that export too may have a perverse factor mix. If the tariff is offset by a change in the exchange rate (r^*) and the effect spread more or less equally across all other tradeable goods, the likelihood of a perverse factor-mix is smaller since the whole pattern of tradeable goods will reflect the perceived notion of relative plentitude and scarcity of the generic factors. The more important is the proportionate input of non-generic factors in a good and the smaller the comparative advantage of one nation in that good (the nearer it is to the dividing line), the greater is the probability that the good will have a perverse mix of generic factors of production. As a general statement, the multiplicity of goods and the possibility of perverse factor-mixes require that the description of the general effect of a tariff on income-distribution avoid the words 'scarce' and 'plentiful' and be explicitly couched in terms of proportionate changes in factor demand.

If Graham's hypothesis of commercial policy formulation is correct, it is reasonable to suppose that the heaviest tariffs will be levied upon type 2 and type 3 goods. Type 2 goods are only likely to have perverse factor mixes to the extent that they use multiple generic factors. Type 3 goods may use industry-specific inputs and are therefore capable of factor-perversity. Type 1 goods, those that are most likely to rely heavily on industry-specific inputs will, with the exception of type $1B$ goods, be less likely to be protected. It might seem, then, that the expected result of tariff imposition on income distribution will be expected to hold. This inference may need qualification to the extent that the exports which are reduced in consequence of the protective measure, are type 1 goods and therefore capable of quite strong factor-perversity.

The Graham hypothesis suggests that if tariff levels are high, the effect of international trade upon the distribution of income (relative to autarky) will depend very directly upon the factor composition used in type 1 goods. Under such conditions, the pattern of demand in international trade could more easily be perverse so that apparently plentiful factors do indeed lose from international trade.

Once the existence of industry-specific factors of production is recognized, the possibility exists that a tariff can generate large proportionate and absolute gains to a single factor. If the industry-specific factor is in inelastic supply in the short run, the increase in its derived demand (the increase in the demand for the finished good) may create quite sizeable rents or quasi-rents.[14] If the long-run supply is more elastic, the gain in income may be reduced over time and, in imperfect factor markets, it is always possible for some cooperating factors to share in the quasi-rents. But, for industry-specific factors, the reason for attempting to gain tariff-protection is quite clear and much clearer than the orthodox theory would suggest. For a corporation or industry, protection may offer quite sizeable increases in short-run profits (and capital gains on the stock exchange). To the extent that a labour union has control over entry into the industrys labour force — even if only by means of demands for a money wage that limits the industry's demand for labour to the number of members in the union — a union can act as if its members were industry-specific even though their skills are in no way special to the industry or different from those of other workers.

Dynamic arguments for protection include senile-industry protection and infant-industry tariff. Senile-industry protection requires a short-run framework since the concept is designed to phase out a senile (or moribund) import-competing industry that, through no fault of its own, has lost its comparative advantage — due either to a movement of r^* or because of an industry-specific disturbance such as the acquisition of technology by a foreign industry.[15] The reason for offering protection to such an industry is that the social costs of letting it contract at the rate dictated by market forces can be unnecessarily high. These costs may derive from the sheer inability of factor markets to absorb the released factors of production (and geographical considerations could be important in such an adjustment) or because the

---

[14] Discussed above in the preceding section.
[15] See my 'Senile-Industry Protection' A Proposal', *Southern Economic Journal* XXXIX, (April 1973), pp. 569–74 for the delineation of the concept. See also Geoffrey E. Wood's 'Comment' and the 'Reply' in *Southern Economic Journal* XLI, (January 1975), pp. 535–41.

industry has industry-specific factors of production which would become worthless if discarded immediately. Consider an industry in a developed nation that is efficient in a free-trade world. Let this industry maintain its overall efficiency enforced by perfect competition in the domestic market. If the industry loses its comparative advantage and returns to scale are approximately constant, the industry could be eliminated extremely quickly — more quickly than the industry-specific physical and human capital employed in the industry could be used up. If the industry-specific physical and human capital are not to be wasted and to be subtracted from society's capital stock, the industry must be protected for it to be phased out. The useful life of the industry is limited to the time needed to reallocate to other industries or to depreciate fully the specific factors used in the industry. Ideally, the industry would be allowed to exhaust its present resources by continuing to produce behind some protective device.[16] What matters also is that the industry not be preserved too long and for this reason, the protection granted should have a finite duration and should decrease as the industry-specific inputs are used up. A pattern, specified in terms of a quota, of progressively reducing protection is shown in figure 10-1. In the figure, C_0 represents the original capacity of the domestic industry at the time it lost competitiveness. The difference between total consumption and domestic production would constitute the original quota, Q_0. Over time, the demand for the good grows at an annual rate of x and the quota is increased so that domestic output reduces to zero in N periods. The number of years over which the industry would benefit from protection would depend upon the characteristics of the specific factors used in the industry and upon the natural rate of depreciation of that capital. The rate of depreciation of the physical capital would be fairly precisely determined. The avoidance of waste of human capital would be less easy. The waste would be reduced if some people were retained in the industry until they could reasonably retire. Other people could be retrained in allied fields. One factor affecting the number of years of protection needed would be

---

[16] This case is not the usual one of an industry asking for protection under the 'escape clause' (GATT Article XIX) since such an industry does not acknowledge its imminent elimination.

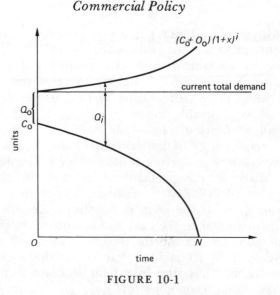

FIGURE 10-1

Determination of the Quota

the degree to which the government was prepared to assist people to retrain or to subsidize early retirement. The explicit recognition of the problem imposed upon industry-specific factors of production when the nation undergoes a change in competitiveness in the activity in which they are engaged, is a useful addition to the analysis of a commercial policy. It makes little difference to the analysis whether the loss of competitiveness of a domestic industry is due to acquisition of technological knowhow by foreign firms or to tariff bargaining under the auspices of the GATT.

The second dynamic argument for tariff protection is also not susceptible to analysis within the orthodox framework. This must surely be a indictment of orthodoxy since the argument for protection of infant industries dates back to the eighteenth century in Alexander Hamilton's *Federalist Papers* and has been used by different nations from that time to the present day. The infant-industry argument is incompatible with orthodoxy because of the explicit need to introduce time into the analysis since the argument hinges upon the generation of a more efficient global resource allocation *in the future* than will evolve naturally. In many ways, the infant-industry argument is the mirror image of the argument for senile-industry protection since both involve finite periods of protection during the adjustment process – the difference is that senile-industry protection is concerned with the phasing out of a dying industry so that the rate of disappearance of the industry is efficient while the infant-industry tariff is concerned with the nursing of a vulnerable industry so that it may eventually achieve independence in a free-trade world.

In the terminology of the generalized theory, the argument for infant-industry protection centres around the role of scalars and modifiers in the production function. In its simplest version, the infant-industry argument avows that the focus nation can produce the good in question more cheaply than foreign industries when the costs are computed on the basis of the input mix element and the prices of factors of production when the scalar is set at some size compatible with efficient plant operation. Thus, the infant-industry argument assumes two things – that economies of scale are the major barrier preventing the development from scratch of a self-sustaining industry and that factor prices in the nation, when that size of operation has been attained, will show the nation to have a comparative advantage in the production of the good. Presumably, most real-world computations are made on the basis of present-day factor costs and the economies of scale achieved by foreign industries. Modifiers can enter into the concept when it is argued that the industry needs time for an evolutionary change in the economy as well as for the growth of the industry to a efficient size. The development of the industry may itself contribute to, as well as benefit from, the development of the economy.

In general, tariffs (and other commercial policy measures) are man-made industry-specific disturbances. As such, the effect of a single tariff will be to alter the shape of the offer curve as well as its position. In the process, the profitability of all closely related and vulnerable industries will be altered. It is for this reason, that a simple theory of commercial policy cannot be generated – because each tariff will have a different set of repercussions even in the absence of retaliation. It follows therefore that the so-called symmetry of export and import taxes is a figment of the orthodox model applicable only under extravagent assumptions.[17]

[17] See Abba P. Lerner, 'The Symmetry between Import and Export Taxes', *Economica* n.s. III (August 1936), pp. 306–13.

Finally, it should be noted that imperfections in international markets due to the existence of cartels and other forms of market power, will have effects that are quite similar to those of commercial policy. The only substantial differences are that the ability to vary relative prices derives from corporate domination rather than from legislative authority and the revenue from the 'tax' goes to the corporation rather than to the government. In addition, the purpose of exploiting market imperfections is to raise revenues (while the purpose of the commercial policy measure is usually its effect upon the pattern of trade) and, by that means, to affect income distribution. Because the system is a price interdependent system, the source of the variation between price and cost is immaterial as far as the effect on the pattern of trade is concerned. What matters in the determination of the volume of trade is the price at which one can purchase from different sources. The perfectly competitive free-trade model is an analytic benchmark which serves as a point of both reference and departure.

11 Two-way Trade

Simultaneous exports and imports of a single good constitute two-way trade for a nation. The quantitative importance of this type of trade pattern is *prima facie* evidence of the inadequacy of the orthodox body of theory to provide a realistic framework for analysis of modern patterns of international trade. This chapter will show how two-way trade can take place between a nation and its trading partners and will identify the main characteristics of the trading nations that will give rise to two-way trade.

The customary name for the phenomenon is 'intra-industry trade'.[1] The preference here for the nomenclature 'two-way' depends on the relatively broad coverage that can intuitively be given to the word 'industry'. For example, the two-digit 'industry' corresponding to the Standard International Trade Classification (SITC) 67 (iron and steel) includes both pig iron (671) and steel pipe fittings (678.5). SITC manufacturing categories are compiled on the basis of the basic raw material involved and can include a very large part of the complete set of vertical stages of processing of that raw material. What is of interest to the student of international trade is why trade should take place in opposite directions in items which are similar in terms of input requirements. Thus, the expression 'intra-industry' can be misleading — particularly to economists not familiar with international trade theory or data sources. The expression 'two-way trade' is more restrictive. Two-way trade is defined as the simultaneous exporting and importing of goods

---

[1] See Bela Balassa, 'Tariff Reductions and Trade in Manufactures among the Industrial Countries', *Americal Economic Review* LVI, (June 1966), pp. 466—73; Herbert G. Grubel, 'Intra-Industry Specialization and the Pattern of Trade', *The Canadian Journal of Economics and Political Science* 33, (August 1967), pp. 374—88; *idem*, 'The Theory of Intra-Industry Trade', in I. A. McDougall and R. H. Snape, (eds.) *Studies in International Economics*, (Amsterdam: North-Holland, 1970), pp. 35—51; and *idem* and Peter J. Lloyd, 'The Empirical Measurement of Intra-Industry Trade', *The Economic Record*, (December 1971), pp. 494—511. The ideas developed in this chapter would not have been possible without these seminal articles.

which use almost identical mixes of inputs (have closely similar production functions) and which serve very similar purposes.

The most obvious cause of the observation of two-way trade in empirical studies is the aggregation within internationally compiled trade categories, of goods that have quite distinct input requirements. Ideally, commodity data on international trade flows would be compiled by production functions and by end-use. Thus goods with the same inputs and the same or similar end-use would be aggregated. Unfortunately, as noted above, the data are instead provided according to the processing of types of raw materials within very broad categories. A spectacular example of this is the exaggeration of Australian two-way trade by the categorical aggregation of gypsum exports to New Zealand, Taiwan and the Philippines and imports of marble from Italy and limestone flux from Japan. Disaggregation by country reduces the volume of such trade and the narrowing of categories will also reduce the volume of two-way trade registered simply by aggregating quite different commodities under the same trade category.[2]

Grubel suggests five causes of two-way trade in homogeneous categories of goods:[3] (*a*) primary products with high transportation costs could result in two-way trade if natural resources were located on opposite sides and at different ends of a long frontier; (*b*) joint production; (*c*) entrepôt trade; (*d*) governmentally produced distortions in prices can create opportunities for entrepreneurs to maximize profits by simultaneously exporting and importing; (*e*) and, fifth, seasonal fluctuations in output or demand.[4] Any of these causes can be reconciled with the existing theory by relatively minor refinements to that theory. Transportation costs can explain the border trade. Economies of joint production will explain banking and insurance and, depending upon the balance-of-payments accounting system, even shipping. Emphasis on value added will explain the entrepôt trade. Government purchases and sales can explain the fourth category. The fifth category can be elimi-

---

[2] Grubel and Lloyd, (*The Economic Record*).

[3] See Grubel, 'The Theory of Intra-Industry Trade', pp. 36–7.

[4] Seasonal fluctuations are related to import calendars mentioned in the preceding chapter. Grubel mentions tourism here but this can only be 'sunlust tourism'. 'Wanderlust tourism' can be intra-industry because it is a non-competitive service and therefore would be a case of categorical aggregation: see my *International Travel: International Trade*, (Lexington, Mass.: Heath Lexington, 1970), pp. 12–21.

nated as two-way trade if the period of analysis is shortened substantially — when electricity is traded because of differences in peak hours on either side of a national boundary and the two power sources are tied into the same grid, this could be explained as temporal variation or as joint production.

The more important causes of two-way trade are likely to involve economies of scale and/or product differentiation. The latter goods are, of course, type 3 goods as described in chapter 3. Economies of scale can cause two-way trade when different goods within the same industry are produced in two countries. Consider an industry comprising two goods, both of which enjoy substantial economies of large-scale production. If both goods had similar input mixes so that they were close to the dividing line, it would be economically efficient for one country to specialize in one of the two goods and to produce it in large quantities and for the second country to produce the second good in large quantities. Each nation would enjoy a comparative advantage in the one good because of its achievement of scale economies.

Product differentiation must be an extremely important cause of two-way trade. Grubel separates the two characteristics of quality differentiation and style differentiation. While it may be useful, conceptually, to separate these two dimensions, and particularly with reference to Linder's hypothesis, the distinction must be blurred beyond recognition in the real world. Linder's hypothesis stressed overlapping incomes as the cause of trade so that quality differences within the same manufactured product would be a straight cause of two-way trade. This reasoning can be supplemented with the effects of skewed income distributions and economies of scale in different models in different countries.[5] Differences in style, design, packaging and even brand names can also account for two-way trade.[6]

The quantitative importance of two-way trade can be seen from the data presented in tables 11-1 and 11-2. Table 11-1 shows the degree to which intra-industry trade existed in 1958 — a ratio of 0.5 is compatible with balanced two-way

[5] See Linder, *An Essay in Trade and Transformation*, and Grubel, 'The Theory of Intra-Industry Trade', pp. 39—43.
[6] Grubel considers technological gaps as causes of intra-industry trade. The generalized theory would submit that this is a separate category and comprises trade in non-competitive goods (type 1C).

TABLE 11-1

Representative Ratios of Trade Balances for 91 Commodity Categories

	Representative ratios of trade balances[a]		
	1958	1963	1968[b]
Belgium	0.458	0.401	0.330
France	0.394	0.323	0.310
Germany	0.531	0.433	0.350
Italy	0.582	0.521	0.373
Netherlands	0.495	0.431	0.375

[a]Calculated as unweighted averages of the ratio of the absolute difference of exports and imports to the sum of exports and imports for 91 industries by the use of the following formula:

$$\left[\frac{1}{n} \Sigma \frac{|X_i - M_i|}{X_i + M_i} \right]$$

where X_i and M_i refer to the intra-EEC exports and imports of commodity category i, and n is the number of the commodity categories considered. If exports or imports predominate completely in any one trade category, that observation will have the value of unity; if trade in all categories were 'one-way', the index would have a value of unity. A decreasing value of the index over time gives evidence of increasing relative importance of two-way trade. As an indication, a ratio of 0.5 is compatible with exports equal to imports (i.e., balanced two-way trade) in *one half* of the industries or with a 75—25 share of the two flows in *all* industries.

[b]The same index based on 79 of Balassa's 91 categories. The smaller sample is caused by a change in data reporting. Computed by the author from OECD, *Trade by Commodities-Market Summaries: Imports—Exports* Series C, (Paris, 1969).

Source: Bala Balassa, *American Economic Review*, (June 1966), p. 471. Balassa's 91 SITC categories were not consistent with regard to the number of digits.

trade in one half of the categories or with a 75—25 share of the two flows in *all* industries. The table also shows how the proportionate importance of two-way trade increased within the European Economic Community in the first decade of the Common Market's existence. While transportation costs, joint production, statistical aggregation, entrepôt trade and seasonal fluctuations could possibly explain the value of the ratios for 1958, the consistent reduction of the ratios in the two subsequent periods must be largely due to the growth of

TABLE 11-2

Australian Intra-industry Trade with Major Trading Partners at Different Levels of Aggregation, 1968—69

Country or country group	Digit level of aggregation				
	7	5	3	2	1
USA	0.968	0.900	0.854	0.750	0.603
UK	0.987	0.958	0.923	0.875	0.685
Japan	0.998	0.978	0.952	0.894	0.820
EEC	0.990	0.968	0.951	0.937	0.847
Canada	0.992	0.928	0.824	0.725	0.614
New Zealand	0.956	0.805	0.695	0.525	0.202
Hong Kong	0.986	0.935	0.867	0.827	0.495
India	0.998	0.982	0.945	0.905	0.505
South Africa	0.993	0.927	0.837	0.697	0.346
South-East Africa	0.985	0.956	0.913	0.912	0.826
Rest of world	0.969	0.894	0.811	0.730	0.480
All countries	0.938	0.851	0.798	0.741	0.571

Notes (1) The smaller the number, the greater the importance of intra-industry trade.

(2) The statistics are global averages for all SITC sections.

(3) Countries are ranked in decreasing order of the value of exports to Australia in 1968—69, except for the remainder groups of South-East Asia and the rest of the world. South-East Asia consists of Brunei, Cambodia, Laos, Malaysia, Indonesia, Philippines, Singapore, Thailand and the Republic of Vietnam.

Source: Grubel and Lloyd; (*The Economic Record*), p. 501.

two-way trade in differentiated products brought about by growth in real incomes and intra-community tariff reductions. Economies of scale achieved in different component items within a trade category could be a contributory factor to the increases but, to the extent that they occurred, they are more likely to have been caused by international production planning by multi-national corporations than by any random process. Table 11-2 is taken from Grubel and Lloyd and shows clearly that, for Australia, ever-finer categorization of commodity classifications will reduce the proportionate importance of intra-industry trade. In fact, Australia is a bad subject for empirical testing of the importance of two-way trade because of the high transportation costs that differentiated goods would

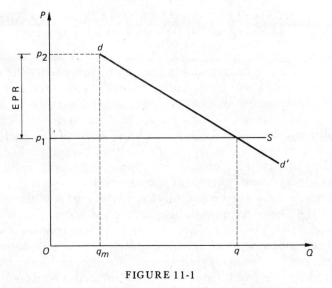

FIGURE 11-1

The Export Price Range

have to overcome. A large proportion of Australian intra-industry trade can be traced to categorical aggregation and to specialization within industries.[7]

Two-way trade in differentiated goods can be explained in terms of the existence of positive 'export price ranges' for competing products in each of two countries. The concept of a positive export price range is given by figure 11.1 (a reproduction of figure 3.2). A positive export price range exists when $p_2 > p_1$.[8] For two-way trade to take place, reciprocal positive 'export price ranges' (EPRs) must exist for competing goods in both countries that produce and consume the category of the good in question. There are several factors that will affect the probability of the existence of reciprocal positive EPRs but all of these can be overcome by a large enough comparative advantage in the 'good' in question.

---

[7] *The Economic Record*, p. 499.
[8] See above, pp. 48–53.

FACTORS AFFECTING THE PROBABILITY OF THE EXISTENCE OF RECIPROCAL EPRs

These are:

(1) The more differentiated the goods, the steeper the slope of the demand curve in both countries and, therefore, the higher, *ceteris paribus*, each p_2. The higher the pair of p_2s, the greater the variation in the two p_1s that can be accommodated simultaneously with reciprocal EPRs. This characteristic of certain commodity groups is very likely to be compatible with the hypothesis put forward by Drèze that specialization in styles, designs, and equipment characteristics (type B goods) is responsible for a significant volume of trade in manufactures.[9] While the Drèze hypothesis also concerned economies of scale in production (and therefore the p_1s), an important aspect of the trade flows was the intrinsic utility attached to 'authentic design' and to the significant degree of differentiation between imported goods and the domestically produced substitute.

(2) The more similar the *per capita* national incomes in the two countries (computed in some international numeraire), the greater the probability that the two p_2s will be approximately the same. The more equal the p_2s, the greater is the probability of two-way trade.

(3) If the two p_1s are very close the probability is high that two-way trade will take place. In a world free of impediments to trade and with production functions with virtually equal technology and little substitutability among factors, the two p_1s will be virtually equal when absolute factor prices are very similar in both countries. This virtual equality of factor prices will most probably occur when *per capita* national incomes are approximately equal.[10] Since competing prices are very influential in the determination of the p_2s and since demand schedules are more likely to be similar in the two countries when *per capita* incomes are similar, it would seem that approximately equal p_1s and approximately equal p_2s will be highly correlated.

Staffan B. Linder hypothesizes that trade will tend to be most intensive between nations with approximately the same

[9] *Recherches économiques de Louvain*, (1961).

[10] Richard N. Cooper, *The Economics of Interdependence*, (New York: McGraw-Hill Co., 1968), ch. 3, suggests that, in fact, this state of affairs has tended to be approached in the Atlantic Community.

levels of *per capita* income since such countries will have similar demand patterns.[11] For Linder, the intensity of trade depends very largely upon the similarity of the quality aspects of demand which derive from the relative sophistication of the consumers. Since demand patterns will overlap, it seems reasonable to suppose that the number of products produced and consumed in the two countries will be a very high proportion of total manufacturers and two-way trade is the more likely on a stochastic basis. Linder does not introduce the differentiation of goods of similar quality and cost into his argument which relies primarily on factor-proportion similarities and economies of scale. Thus two-way trade will be most common betwen manufacturing nations of approximately equal incomes and factor prices. The presence of large differences in the endowment of land, minerals or other non-reproducible resources will diminish the possibility of two-way trade much as it will diminish the likelihood of approximate equality of incomes.

(4) In addition to two-way trade in final differentiated goods, two-way trade can also take place in intermediate goods. Two-way trade in intermediate goods is likely to prerequire the same general conditions for the existence of reciprocal EPRs as final goods: approximate equality of incomes and of factor prices, and/or significant differentiation among competing goods. 'Afterbusiness' or spare parts for previously exported goods will enjoy a very high degree of product differentiation and may help to explain the comparative slowness with which international geographic patterns of trade respond to relative price changes. Similarly, technologically based or design-oriented differentiation in intermediate goods will enjoy quite steeply sloped demand curves and can create two-way trade by counteracting a cost advantage in foreign nations for substitutes with much the same input mix.

(5) *Ceteris paribus*, the smaller tariff rates and transportation costs, the more likely the two p_1s will be approximately the same, and therefore, the greater the probability of the existence of reciprocal EPRs. Subsidization of domestic industry is equivalent, in this respect, to a tax on imports. Clearly, mutual reductions in tariffs can increase the volume of two-way trade.

[11] *An Essay on Trade and Transformation*, (New York: John Wiley and Sons, 1961), pp. 94—109.

(6) For any demand curve, p_2 depends upon the magnitude of x_{min}. In so far as different industries have different sales-distribution organizations, x_{min} will vary for different types of goods. The more simple the sales operation or the more easily the selling process of imports combines with existing sales outlets, the smaller will be x_{min} and the greater the probability, *ceteris paribus*, of two-way trade. Where multi-national corporations have existing sales complexes already set up for their own domestically produced goods, the imported differentiated product will be likely to need only a very small minimum quantity.

The gains from international trade in differentiated goods are to be found in the wider choice offered to consumers in the different nations, in the possibilities of an 'exchange' of scale economies among nations and, perhaps the most important benefit of all, increased competition in the domestic markets. This exposure of domestic industry to foreign competition can take two forms: a reduction in the degree of market imperfection in the industry in the importing nation and the diminution in entrepreneurial lethargy in the domestic firms. These gains must exceed any net burden of quasi-rents reaped by the exporting country (in the case of imports) or repatriated as profits when direct investment has taken place for the importing or host nation to benefit. Gains or losses may derive from the production plans of multi-national corporations and their transfers of intermediate goods among affiliates. The potential for national gain exists when the domestic affiliate enjoys a preferred position and supplies other affiliates in nearby countries. The potential for national loss exists when a foreign subsidiary is supplying the domestic affiliate. Where Coase-type internal economies exceed national comparative advantage or disadvantage, the multi-national corporation becomes the arbitrary decider of production location and a nation may 'win' or 'lose' in the process. Under such conditions it is difficult to speak of the 'gain from trade' in the usual meaning of that phrase. Certainly the average gain from trade in differentiated goods will be smaller than that achieved by the exportation and importation of non-competitive or homogeneous goods in accordance with comparative advantage.[12]

[12] See Grubel, *The Canadian Journal of Economics and Political Science* (August 1967), pp. 386–7 and see also R. G. Lipsey, 'The Theory of Customs Unions: A General Survey', *Economic Journal*, (September 1960), pp. 496–513 and reprinted

International trade in differentiated goods fits easily into the generalized theory. The balance of trade on type 3 goods will, with balanced total trade or current account, be offset by countervailing balances on homogeneous or non-competitive goods. To the extent that trade in type 3 goods involves a producer's surplus in that the export price includes a return to proprietary knowledge or even to 'being in business', an increase in the balance on type 3 goods will improve the nation's single factoral terms of trade. But, because different goods may have different rates of surplus, it is not necessarily true that a positive balance of trade in differentiated goods means a greater producer's surplus than that enjoyed by the trading partner.

An increase in foreign demand for a nation's differentiated good or goods will be likely to react back unfavourably upon the export sales and profitability of exporters of homogeneous and non-competitive goods. This effect will be instigated by an appreciation of the currency of the focus nation and will induce an upward shift in the dividing line. The further impact upon factor markets will depend upon the comparability of the mix of factors employed by the expanding differentiated-goods industry and that of the contracting exporting industries.

Finally, the existence of two-way trade in differentiated goods will qualify the traditional analysis of the process of adjustment to some specified trade disturbance. The ensuing analysis assumes given tastes, resource endowments, production functions, design features and a network of multi-national corporations (although no specific reference to dividend repatriation is included). For simplicity, an equilibrium frame of reference is used to show how the long-run effects of a disturbance will influence the short-run reactions.

Figure 11-2 depicts the international equilibrium (in a two-country world) of a differentiated goods firm located in country A. The figure bears some resemblance to the monopolistic-composition model of the large-group case but it is assumed that each firm in the industry has a perfectly elastic supply curve at the going administered or equilibrium price in domestic currency. The use of dual demand curves enables the reaction of market shares and of sales to be analyzed when imports change their prices and domestic firms do not. For this

in Caves and Johnson, *Readings in International Economics*, pp. 261–78. This point is always subject to the X-efficiency implications for the import-competing industry.

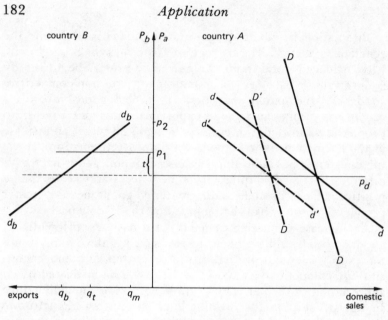

FIGURE 11-2

The International Equilibrium of *A*'s Differentiated Product

purpose the three *dd* curves should be interpreted as showing the demand for the firm's products when all of *A*'s firms change their prices and *B*'s firms do not change theirs. The *DD* curve in *A* shows the sensitivity of the firm's sales in *A* when all competitors regardless of the country of origin alter their prices equally with the firm in question. The diagram allows for quality and design differences in the position of the demand schedules. The firm sells at price p_d in country *A* and at p_1 in country *B* where p_1 is equal to p_d plus the existing tariff.[13] (For simplicity, the existence of quasi-rents is disregarded).

When economic integration causes the bilateral elimination of tariffs, imported differentiated goods become cheaper in both countries. *A*'s firm's exports increase along $d_b d_b$ as the price in *B* falls from p_1 to p_d: the increase in exports is $q_b - q_t$. This adjustment assumes that domestic prices by all competitors (in both *A* and *B*) do not change in response to integration. In *A*, the firm's sales decline as its 'share of the market' curve

---

[13] Neither transportation costs nor selling costs are considered here.

shifts from DD to $D'D'$ in response to the decreased price of imports. The adjustments in the two markets tend to be mutually offsetting for all firms as export increases counteract foreign encroachments in the domestic market. There must exist a pair of foreign and domestic price elasticities such that no change in the total output of the firm will result from the bilateral elimination of tariffs. The offsetting characteristic of the process reduces the probability that competing firms will change their domestic prices.[14]

If the firm depicted in figure 11-2 is now assumed to be representative of all of A's differentiated industry, the impact of the existence of two-way trade in differentiated products on the general process of balance-of-payments adjustment can be examined. Assume a change in tastes for homogeneous goods such that the terms of trade turn against A and a depreciation of A's currency is required. This example is analogous to the need for adjustment that could result from economic integration.

In terms of figure 11-2, a depreciation of A's currency will reduce p_1 in B and, in the absence of any retaliatory price adjustments by competitors in B, lead to an increase in exports along $d_b d_b$. Domestically, more expensive import competition will shift both DD and $d_a d_a$ to the right (not shown) by an amount determined by the elasticity of demand in A for B's differentiated goods — the prices of A's goods being held constant in domestic currency. The two effects will be self-reinforcing. The sensitivity of net exports of differentiated goods will depend upon the elasticities of demand, upon the possibility and magnitude of any discretionary or administered price reduction by B's industries in response to their loss of sales, and upon any change in costs in the two countries induced by changes in relative factor prices caused in turn by the change in the output mix.

The introduction of differentiated goods will presuppose greater sensitivity of the trade balance to depreciation if the demand (and supply) elasticities of exports and imports of

---

[14] It may have been that with the prospect of further tariff reductions within EEC nations, new differentiated products entered into two-way trade within the periods analyzed because, in anticipation of these reductions, x_{min} would become very small. This would tend to emphasize the expansion of two-way trade in the initial years of integration.

differentiated goods are likely to exceed the equivalent elasticities of homogeneous goods. Even if two-way trade does not take place in a differentiated good, trade in import-competing differentiated products will react to a depreciation along a *dd* curve rather than along a *DD* curve and may, therefore, be expected to be biased toward a relatively high elasticity. Where two-way trade does exist, there is an obvious bias toward differentiated goods having greater relative sensitivity to depreciation than homogeneous goods. A homogeneous good reacts to depreciation along only one demand curve – a differentiated good has two demand curves. Thus if the sum of the elasticities of the two relevant *dd* curves exceeds the average elasticity of demand of homogeneous goods, the adjustment mechanism can be considered likely to be more sensitive as a result of the introduction of two-way trade into the model.[15]

The degree of any increase in the sensitivity of the adjustment mechanism to the existence of trade in differentiated goods will depend upon the ratio of the value of trade in differentiated goods to the total value of trade as well as on the relative elasticities of demand and upon changes in money costs of production measured in domestic currencies. In addition to providing the weights applicable to the elasticities of the individual categories of types of goods, the ratio of two-way trade to total trade may be important because of the probable positive relationship between the magnitude of the ratio and the weighted elasticity coefficient for differentiated goods. Given the importance of the degree of product differentiation in the probability that reciprocal EPRs will exist for a good, minimal two-way trade may be expected to comprise largely distinctively differentiated goods which have relatively steeply sloped demand curves in foreign nations (type *B*). Randomly, the steeper the slope of the demand curve, the smaller will be the expected value of the coefficient of elasticity. As the proportion of trade in differentiated goods increases, less well-differentiated goods will come to be traded in two directions and the weighted average elasticity of demand will be likely to become larger.

[15] Supply elasticities have not been considered here. To avoid any confusion, it should be mentioned that the question of whether or not the introduction of differentiated goods increases the sensitivity of the system to a depreciation, refers only to abstract models and is not intended to suggest that two-way trade is, in some way, separable from other trade.

The degree to which the balance of trade of a nation engaging in significant proportionate amounts of two-way trade, will be more sensitive to currency depreciation and therefore require less internal reallocation of resources in response to a given external disturbance, is not only determined by the elasticities of demand for internationally traded goods. The pattern of expenditure switching and its impact upon the levels of domestic demand and the supply elasticities of individual goods are also important. To the extent that type A or type B goods have high income elasticities, the effect of the greater expected demand elasticities of differentiated goods will be enhanced. Similarly, if differentiated goods do testify to the presence of a wide range of goods with quite similar input mixes being traded internationally, and if these goods are produced under conditions of constant returns to scale, supply elasticities can also be expected to be quite high.

CONCLUSION

Differentiated products are probably important elements in the existence of two-way trade though other possible causes should not be disregarded. Certainly, differentiated products can explain the observed increase in two-way trade in the EEC countries in the first ten years of the Community's existence. It is possible that the growth of trade in differentiated products has reduced the costs of adjustment that must accompany the integration process and, in that way, has contributed significantly to the welfare gains from integration. However, the major welfare gains that can be achieved by trade in differentiated products result from gains in X-efficiency.[16] An increased proportion of two-way trade testifies to the existence of trade in differentiated goods and should heighten the sensitivity of the trade balance to currency depreciation.[17]

Finally, the identification of two-way trade with differentiated, manufactured products tends to qualify two propo-

[16] W. S. Comanor and H. Leibenstein, 'Allocative Efficiency, X-Efficiency and the Measurement of Welfare Losses', *Economica* n.s., (August 1969), pp. 304–309.

[17] The fact that differentiated goods prices are administratively fixed and well advertised may mean that these prices in foreign currency will not adjust immediately with a change in the rate of exchange and that they will be likely to be immune from any changes in the broadening of the band of exchange-rate flexibility around the par value.

sitions in so far as developing nations are concerned. First, Linder's hypothesis that the volume of trade in manufactures with different trading partners will vary positively with the similarity of *per capita* incomes,[18] must be limited to developed nations with predominant manufacturing sectors. Secondly, Grubel's proposition that 'it is advantageous to proceed toward trade liberalization *via* the formation of customs unions among countries at similar levels of development'[19] must be qualified for countries in the process of developing their manufacturing sectors. It is not immediately apparent that involvement in two-way trade with other countries in similar stages of development is a worthwhile goal for a developing nation. The X-efficiency gains are likely to be small when competition is opened up between manufacturing concerns in developing nations. The gain from uniting developing nations at similar low levels of *per capita* income would come from the ability more easily to achieve economies of scale of production by planning the integration of scale economies. There will be little loss of payments vulnerability for developing nations through integration, particularly if the developing nations as a whole suffer from payments vulnerability with the developed world.

---

[18] *An Essay on Trade and Transformation*, p. 95.
[19] *The Canadian Journal of Economics and Political Science*, p. 387.

12 Conclusion

The development of a more general theory of international trade and resource allocation has been designed to serve two purposes. The first of these is destructive: to rid the existing corpus of economic thought of an overly refined and excessively simple orthodoxy in international economic theory. The second purpose is constructive: to provide a general and flexible but realistic frame of reference to serve as a basis for analyses of international economic phenomena.

The restrictiveness of the institutional and behavioural assumptions underlying the orthodox model is quite clear. Whether one defines orthodoxy in the extreme version in which factor price equalization has already taken place or in the less extreme version characterized by the assumptions of Meade's *Geometry* with the additional proviso that neither nation specializes in the production of a single good, the orthodox model fails to provide an analytical basis for many current as well as long-established problems in international economics.[1] Some of these topics can be identified by the chapter titles in Part Two: colonialism; factor migration; multi-national enterprise; commercial policy; and two-way or intra-industry trade. An analysis of any of these topics has required a separate and partial-analysis approach that relates only tangentially, if at all, to the orthodox model. This state of affairs is not peculiar to international economics and extends over a wide range of topics which have micro-theoretic bases.[2] Some attempts have

---

[1] See, *inter alia*, Gunner Myrdal, *Rich Lands and Poor* (New York: Harper and Row, 1957), pp. 117–62. Despite Dr. Myrdal's distinction and the recognition of that distinction with a Nobel prize, it is probably true to say that his thinking has had little effect upon the thinking of mainstream economists. It may be that his failure significantly to influence orthodox economic thinking derives from his failure to provide an alternative framework for rigorous analysis. As an example, see his approach in *Asian Drama*, pp. 8 and 12: '. . . [W]hat I have reached for in this book, beyond mere criticism, is a tentative "theory", one that co-ordinates in a systematic manner a general conception of what is happening in the region of South Asia'. 'From a scientific point of view, a more essential function of studies following a generalizing approach is to provide a logically correlated system of questions to be answered by further research, a "theory" in other words.'

[2] See Shubik, *Journal of Economic Literature* (June 1970), pp. 4, 6, 7.

been made to incorporate some of the problems or short-comings listed above into the orthodox model. Consider, for example, the integration of tariffs into the general equilibrium solution of the orthodox theory. The basic theory has been adapted with great skill to allow for a duty to be applied to an import and the solution to the system worked out to examine its sensitivity to different elasticities of substitution in consumption and of transformation in production. But such theorizing grafts a real-world phenomenon artificially on to an existing abstract theory. It does not broaden the core theory's ability to serve as a basis for the analysis of such problems as tariff bargaining, the implications of different tariff structures, or the usefulness of tariffs in the process of economic development.[3] The result is equivalent to saying – if the world did exist as our theory portrays it, what would be the effect of nations imposing tariffs on the importation of foreign goods? There is one final dimension that deserves explicit recognition. The orthodox theory has the traditional *wertfrei* approach. This approach requires the theory to be indifferent to the distribution of income among the participants in the theory. It makes little sense in a world in which sovereign nation states are concerned with little else.

This criticism of orthodoxy should not be interpreted as implying a lack of respect for economists who have contributed to the development of the orthodox model or for the quality of those contributions as pieces of economic analysis. There is difference of opinion about the purpose of economics and about methodology. But even more important is the fact that the generalized theory is, like its macroeconomic predecessor,[4] a clear example of 'on the shoulders of giants'. It would not be possible to develop a generalized theory without being able to use works of predecessors as platforms from which to see further and as the raw material for the synthesis that is the generalized theory. These predecessors include adherents to orthodoxy such as Jones and Samuelson, critics such as

---

[3] Consequently, Raul Prebisch has, like Myrdal, failed to leave a lasting impact upon international economic theory. Prebisch might have been able to be more influential among North American economists and perhaps less influential among Latin American policymakers had he seen fit to confront orthodoxy with an alternative specific frame of reference.

[4] See the preface to my *An Aggregate Theory of International Payments Adjustment* (London: Macmillan, 1974).

Leontief and Ohlin, extenders such as Kenen and Vernon and iconoclasts such as Graham and Linder.

What does the generalized theory provide? The basic framework of the generalized theory is a price-interdependent model of international linkages in both product and factor markets. By broadening the set of underlying data on which the model is built to include different kinds of factors with varying degrees of mobility it has been made possible for any partial equilibrium analysis to be related to the larger and general frame of reference. The introduction of industry-specific factors and of scalars and modifiers to the production function permit the incorporation into the generalized theory of any disturbance that can be analyzed in a two-country framework. When the disturbance analyzed to an appropriate degree of complexity in partial equilibrium, is incorporated into the generalized theory, the direction of the changes in the complete set of prices that are the consequences of the original disturbance, will be given. Presumably, any potentially disruptive or damaging consequences that will be transmitted to other sectors can be analyzed in greater detail and fed back into the price-interdependent system.

The generalized theory is designed expressly to be able to incorporate the sequential nature of local disturbance and general consequence. The theory is set in a period-analysis or short-run framework that insists that analysts consider the time-sequence of any problem. This approach has two obvious virtues: it emphasizes concern for the short-run *and* for any disparities between the short-run and long-run equilibria; it avoids the deadening effect of general equilibrium with all of the timelessness that this analytic approach must possess. In the real world, disturbances are, almost always, local in origin (in a market or geographic sense) and then they spread out into different areas. Just as the disequilibrium version of period analysis implies, other sectors and areas are protected from the disturbance in the short run by the use of inventories as buffers.[5] Another advantage of the short-run framework is that disturbances do not come in a tidy sequence nor do they necessarily come singly. If economic analysis has, through the roughly two centuries of its existence, one paramount weakness

---

[5] See Baumol, *Economic Dynamics*, pp. 130–4.

it has been its unwillingness to recognize the inevitability of disturbances impinging upon the economic system. The approach has been to consider an economic disturbance as a special event rather than as a member of a sequence of stochastic events. This concept of the world has given to economic policy-making a literally reactionary cast. The approach emphasizes the concept of a state of normalcy which will be interrupted on occasion instead of emphasizing a state of disequilibrium battered by a continual stream of disrupting forces of varying importance and benificence. The desirability of having policy-makers and analysts imbued with an attitude that regards the economic system as disturbance-prone is probably more desirable in international economics than in any other branch of the discipline because of the much greater number of potential sources of disturbance.

Appendix: Environmental Protection and International Trade Theory

Professor Ingo Walter is the undisputed leader in analyses of the impact of environmental controls on the pattern of international trade and on the implications of such controls for direct international investment.[1] While the whole question of the impact of the introduction of environmental control on the pattern of trade is sensitive to the manner in which the controls are impososed — by Pigovian taxes or by direct subsidy — and to the degree to which environmental protection measures serve as a cloak for the introduction of non-tariff barriers against foreign-made goods, the basic analysis can be usefully developed in terms of the generalized theory. This is the purpose of the appendix. It is arguable that the analytic problems encountered by Walter would have been more tractable had the generalized theory been available for use in their solution since the analysis requires a multi-commodity, multi-factor model that allows for a potentially exhaustible stock of one factor.

Walter distinguishes three functional sources of environmental despoilation.[2]

Type A: Final and intermediate goods and raw materials which when used as intended damage the environment — automobiles, pesticides, detergents, jet aircraft are among these goods. This type of pollution stems from a consumption process.

[1] See 'Environmental Control and Patterns of International Trade and Investment: An Emerging Policy Issue', Banca Nazionale del Lavoro *Quarterly Review* (March 1972), pp. 82—106; 'The Pollution Content of American Trade', *Western Economic Journal* XI (March 1973), pp. 61—70; 'Pollution and Protection: U.S. Environmental Controls as Competitive Distortions', *Weltwirtschaftliches Archiv* 110 (Heft 1 1974), pp. 104—13; and 'International Trade and Resource Diversion: The Case of Environmental Management', *Weltwirtschaftliches Archiv* 110 (Heft 3 1974), pp. 482—93. This Appendix relies heavily on Walter's work.

[2] Banca Nazionale del Lavoro *Quarterly Review* (March 1972), p. 84.

Type B: Residuals of the consumption process — products which are discarded in a manner harmful to the environment. Waste disposal can be included here or under type *C*.

Type C: Residuals of the production process — the side effects of production which damage the environment. Waste products would be important among the goods included in this category and for this reason the waste of humans can more easily be incorporated in production pollution.

Controls designed to reduce consumption—pollution will need to reduce the amount of consumption of pollutant-generating activities or to penalize the act of polluting in such a way that the inputs into consumption processes are changed. Thus, measures designed to reduce type *A* and type *B* pollution will, in so far as they are successful, alter the mix of consumption in a nation. The greater the concern with the preservation of the environment, the greater is the change in the pattern of consumption likely to be. In this way, the introduction of measures to prevent environmental despoilation (or an increase in them) will alter the pattern of international trade through a change in demand for some imports and a change in the availability of supply of some exports. This effect is conceptually straightforward and is analogous in trade theory to a change in tastes or even to change in commercial policy. Type *C* pollution, the side effects of production processes, can be assumed to be controlled or reduced by the application to all production processes of an effluent fee or charge. The principle of an effluent fee poses many problems of measurement and enforcement but it is generally accepted to be the most efficient of all measures designed to achieve a rational trade-off between pollution and real costs of material absorption forgone.[3] The effluent fee equalizes at the margin the social disutility brought on by different kinds of pollution and the monetary costs of reducing the volume of pollutants. In this way, the cost to society of environmental despoilation is internalized into the market mechanism and the social cost of pollutants generated in the course of production is passed on to the user of the good or service in the form of a higher money price. Any system of measures that alters the relative and absolute costs of goods

[3] See J. J. Seneca and M. K. Taussig, *Environmental Economics* (New York: Prentice-Hall, 1974), pp. 79—87.

produced within a nation will reinforce the effects on the pattern of trade of type *A* and type *B* pollution controls.

The use of the generalized theory as a basis for analysis of the imposition of pollution controls on international trade patterns requires the introduction of a sixth category of factor of production. This factor of production can be called 'environmental assimilative capacity' or 'pollution assimilative capacity'. In a *laissez-faire* economy this factor of production has a zero price and is therefore not included in the resource allocation process. When assimilative capacity is priced, the pattern of international trade and production will respond according to the importance of that factor in the production (and consumption) of different goods and according to the different prices of that factor in different nations.

Equation $(5-1)^4$ showed the determination of the money price of the ith good and this price was the basis for the ranking of goods by comparative advantage. The imposition of a (positive) price on environmental assimilative capacity, e, requires that this input be included in the pricing or cost equations:

$$p_i = a_{ik} \cdot p_k + a_{i1} \cdot p_1 + a_{ih} \cdot p_h + a_{ir} \cdot p_r + a_{ip} \cdot p_p + a_{ie} \cdot p_e \tag{A-1}$$

The price, p_e, must be an administratively determined price. Since there exist many types of pollutants with varying potential for damaging the environment, p_e will consist of a set of prices. The more damaging the individual type of pollutant the greater is the assimilative capacity that it will 'use up' and the greater will be its price. (This concept of multiple pricing for a factor of production has its equivalent in the non-generic factors h, r and p.) The varying relative prices of the different types of pollution will be determined with reference to a general or absolute price that will be determined by the marginal rate of social substitution of environmental preservation for material goods. The richer the country and the greater the environmental despoilation that has already taken place, the greater is the absolute price, p_e, likely to be.

Equation (A-1) will serve as the basis for determining the ranking by comparative advantage if the effluent fee is actually

---

[4] See p. 93 above.

paid. Since the idea of the fee is to encourage manufacturers (and others) to reduce the generation of pollutants, it is likely that many will not pay the fee but will adapt their production processes instead. The adaption of the production process will involve either the payment of a smaller fee or of no fee at all. But the reduction of pollution generation will alter the quantities used of the other factors of production and, through that, will change the relative prices of different factors of production. As soon as an effluent fee is imposed p_i will change whether or not the fee is actually paid.

The imposition of an effluent fee or a change in p_e will bring about a change in comparative advantage for virtually all goods. It will therefore cause, simultaneously, both a change in shape and a shift of the national offer curve. Even in the absence of a change in the foreign effluent fee, there will be an induced shift in the shape and position of the foreign offer curve. A change in the set of relative prices embodied in p_e will be likely to cause what is predominantly an industry-specific disturbance and a change in the general price, p_e, will cause what is mainly a general disturbance.

International trade in goods with pollution content will allow supplies of environmental assimilative capacity to be exchanged among nations in the same way that international trade involves the exchange of other factors of production. Nations with a high p_e will import pollution-intensive goods from countries with a low p_e and a correspondingly plentiful endowment of environmental assimilative capacity. Assume, reasonably, that p_e will be positively correlated with *per capita* national income [5] and that below some level of *per capita* national income, p_e will be set at zero. [6] Under quite simple assumptions such as these it is possible to make some indications of the probable pattern of international trade that follows on the introduction of an effluent fee in different nations.

As indicated by equation (A-1), the imposition of an effluent fee will alter the ranking by comparative advantage of the various goods. But the degree of the pre-effluent fee advantage will be important in determining the new ranking since the effluent

---

[5] Oil producing and exporting nations may be excepted here.

[6] The sheer intensity of demand for material goods and the relatively low levels of type C pollution in poor countries will rationalize the zero price on environmental assimilative capacity in these countries.

fee is merely one input among six. The greater the sensitivity of any particular good to a change in r^* the greater is its potential sensitivity to the imposition of effluent fees. Trade in manufactured goods in which international cost differences tend to be small and supply elasticities high, can be expected to be quite sensitive to the levels of and to changes in p_e in different nations. This sensitivity will will be reinforced for trade in some consumer-durable items if consumption charges are imposed on type A pollution simultaneously. Given the importance of the internal combustion engine in international trade and its contribution to environmental despoilation, the magnitude of the effect of effluent fees upon the pattern of trade and upon industry prosperity in different countries could be quite impressive. Almost inevitably, sizeable disturbances of this kind will lead to overt protection (under GATT Article XIX) or to covert protective measures in the form of non-tariff barriers. The potential disruptiveness following from the imposition of environmental protective measures suggests that such measures should be introduced very gradually and, optimally, with some degree of co-operation among the manufacturing nations.[7]

The direct impact of effluent fees upon the pattern of trade will be mitigated by the change in r^* that will accompany any disturbance. A nation increasing its level of effluent fees unilaterally will experience an adverse shift in its terms of trade and a decrease in its r^*. Thus, the marginal export may not lose its export market if its increase in money costs and the proportionate depreciation are approximately equal.

The redistribution of production of pollution-causing goods among developed nations will depend largely upon the disparity in the general levels of effluent fees among nations. Given that poor nations will not impose any fees, the redistribution of trade among rich nations is likely to be small in comparison with the rearrangement of trading patterns between the bloc of rich and the bloc of poor nations. The concern of rich nations with the preservation of their finite stock of environmental

---

[7] What is suggested here is that the structure of effluent fees would be set individually by nations and a target level of p_e would also be set. However, nations would agree to approach that target level gradually — each nation approaching its target level by the same percentage per annum. This dimension of international co-operation has domestic aspects that coincide with international actions and is the more likely to be instituted for this reason.

assimilative capacity and the relative plenitude of that factor in poor nations suggests that poor (or semi-developed) nations will enjoy much greater opportunities to sell manufactured goods to rich countries.[8] This will improve the terms of trade of the poor bloc with the rich bloc and can be expected to be generally beneficial to the development process.

This redistribution of international trade flows will obey the pattern indicated by money costs and prices. While it is inevitable that a sizeable increase in p_e in one group of nations and not in another will lead to an increase in imports of goods with a large a_e, the size of the a_{ie} is not the sole determinant of the change in comparative advantage. The availability of other factors (as well as the change in r^*) will also be important. The availability of co-operating factors of production will depend upon the factor supply functions in the poor nations. Some products are likely to require industry-specific proprietary knowledge and human capital that are not available in poor countries. The result of the imposition of effluent fees in rich countries will be to create very great incentives for direct foreign investment in poor nations.[9] The corollary of an industry-specific outflow of productive capacity will be a serious decrease in the demand for generic and industry-specific factors in that industry in the rich country — quite possibly of the magnitude experienced by the Union of Electrical, Radio and Machine Workers in the United States as a result of the relocation of television and electronic manufacturing outside the United States in the late 'sixties.[10]

There is a further dimension to this problem that may invalidate the assumption of zero fees in poor nations. Environmental assimilative capacity is a particular type of natural resource. It is internationally immobile and is therefore capable of earning a rent for its owners. Since assimilative capacity may be termed a public good or a public asset, any rent earned by such an asset should accrue to the indigenous people of the nation. The governments of nations exporting pollution-creating goods should consider the desirability of

---

[8] Subject always to the institution of strict commercial-policy restrictions.

[9] See Walter, Banca Nazionale del Lavoro *Quarterly Review*, p. 91. This does not preclude the erection of mobility-braking forces either by the rich or the poor nations.

[10] See *The Economics of Business Investment Abroad*, pp. 201–4.

imposing an effluent fee upon exports of goods so that the rent will accrue to those people whose asset is being used up in the provision of exports.[11] The level of the effluent fee to be charged will be determined in a different way from in a rich country. In the poor country, the level of the fee will be determined by the comparative advantage enjoyed by the poor countries achieved by setting the fee at zero. The purpose of the fee is to maximize the nation's gain from trade. There is, of course, a danger that the poor nations will compete away this potential rent and a cartel arrangement might benefit developing nations. It is of paramount importance that an effluent fee be levied upon exports of foreign subsidiaries because if no fee is levied, the return to the environmental assimilative capacity will accrue to the foreign corporation.

Finally, the concern with preservation of environmental assimilative capacity will lead to a great deal of research into means by which pollution can be reduced. The industry-specific proprietary knowledge engendered in this way may slow down the transfer of productive capacity to poor countries, might even allow a nation with a higher p_e to export (some) goods with an erstwhile high pollution content or may lead to the existence of non-competitive exports to other manufacturing nations, or even to the subsidiaries located in poor countries.

---

[11] The rent here is identical to that earned by other types of natural resources — the fee will internalize the rent. Further, it does not mean, as it would in a rich country, that the proceeds of the tax would be devoted to recreation or preservation of environmental assimilative capacity.

Index

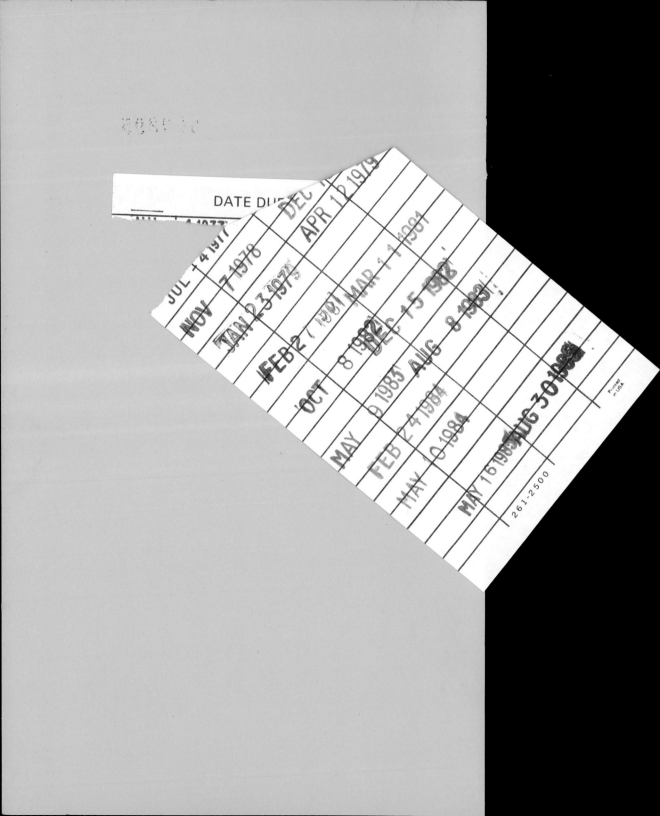